MW01593537

TEACHING:

AN *UNAUTHORIZED* GUIDE TO SURVIVING THE PROFESSION

By

CATHERINE B. WARD and BRYAN W. BREESE

Keep up the fight!

Bryan Breese

Catherine B Ward

Ward Creative Group Publishing

Text copyright ©2013
Ward Creative Group
All Rights Reserved

To teachers everywhere

Table of Contents

Chapter Contents

INTRODUCTION

If you are in an education program at any nice university, you have undoubtedly been surrounded by positive, gregarious, enthusiastic people. Why? Because they are NOT school teachers. They are people who *want* to be teachers, or worse yet, people who think they can teach people how to *be* teachers.

Don't worry. This is not another book about how to be a good teacher. You've likely had a bounty of instruction in that area. Also, please be aware that there is no data in this book. There is nothing tested, standardized, normed, averaged or otherwise datafied. Teaching is an art, not a science. If you like data, go into accounting. Teachers, real teachers, don't *do* data. Central Office people like data because it makes their jobs seem necessary and valuable. We all know it is twaddle and we will spend no further time on it.

So, why this book? We are not interested in making a mark on education. We are not interested in fame or fortune (unless it involves lottery winnings). This is a book about how to survive, and we are simply interested in doing something that hasn't been done very well so far—telling the truth, the truth about public education and the teaching profession. Sometimes the truth is uncomfortable. But we know the truth when we write it. We know because we've been down and dirty with the troops for over 28 years. We've been in the trenches and we know the strategies for survival. Yes, we're bitter; but get used to it—everybody who has been in education for more than fifteen minutes is. The pay puts us at the bottom of the middle class, the expectations are outrageous, and the vast majority of educators are no damn fun. Sadly, many people with whom you will work are horrible, and you will have to spend a lot of time and energy ignoring them in order to last very long in this career. It is, without a doubt, a complete waste of your student loans and five years of higher education.

That being said, this book is intended neither to discourage, nor, God forbid, to encourage anyone (especially our own children) to go into the field. If you want to be a teacher, hey, that's your business. But we want you to go in with eyes open and expectations low. You will be a lot happier that way. For the purposes of this text real-life stories have been included—in the world of educational leadership, this is called anecdotal evidence—but we don't care. We just like to tell stories about the bizarre and often hideous world of teaching. We have changed all the names to protect the innocent/guilty. In the text to follow, the "we" refers to both of us and the "I" refers to Catherine B. Ward unless otherwise noted.

If you've maintained interest enough to read the entire introduction, then by all means, carry on. Forge ahead. Enjoy. Also, it's supposed to be funny.

Catherine B. Ward
Bryan W. Breese

CHAPTER 1: DO YOU HAVE WHAT IT TAKES TO TEACH?

Teaching is one of the few professional jobs that just about everybody thinks they can do. We do not agree. Take our little quiz, tally your score, and then decide.

Teacher Quiz

1. It's a beautiful Sunday afternoon in the fall. You:

    a. wash the car, take a drive, make a barbecue picnic in the park

    b. dream up clever lesson plans to engage and enlighten your students

    c. grade papers

    d. watch football, drink tequila, and pray for a freak snowstorm

2. Does your last name rhyme with a body part, bodily function, or slang term for a body part or bodily function?

    a. No, but it does rhyme with smart.

    b. Oh my Lord, it does!

    c. I don't think so.

    d. No, thank goodness, no.

3. How long do you need in the bathroom?

    a. My bathroom habits are none of your business.

    b. 5-10 minutes

    c. 2-5 minutes

    d. I can pee, change my tampon, and fix my lipstick in less than 90 seconds.

4. Which of the following lifestyle goals most closely matches yours?

    a. I am married to someone who makes a nice living. I don't really need to teach; I do it because I love it.

    b. I'd like to own a nice house on a tree-lined street and drive a nice car. I'd like to retire someplace warm and sunny, maybe a beach house in North Carolina.

    c. I'd like to own my own townhouse or condo. I have plenty of credit cards and not all of them are maxed out.

    d. I'd like to drive a 10 year old car and live in a house half the size of the vast majority of my students. I enjoy eating beans and rice the last two weeks of the month. I plan to maintain student loans older than my car. My mother is willing to buy my kids all of their back-to-school clothes.

5. Which of the following expressions best describes your personal flexibility?

    a. rigid, like granite

    b. I'll bend, but I won't break; I'm like Gumby.

    c. I go with the flow better than the Mississippi River.

    d. When asked to take one in the tail pipe, I bend right over and grab my ankles.

6. How many years are you willing to wear your current wardrobe?

    a. My clothes say a lot about who I am; I should always look my best and that means keeping up with current styles.

    b. While I don't really follow fashion, I do think it's important to look professional.

    c. five to seven years

    d. Clothes, like teeth, are meant to last a lifetime.

7. Which of the following statements made by students is true?

    a. "My book is in my boyfriend's locker, and he's in gym right now and they're outside on the soccer field, so I won't be able to read in class today."

    b. "I emailed you my paper last night. I don't know, though, because my dad's computer has been giving him some real trouble lately."

    c. "We had an assignment due today?"

    d. "I hate this class."

8. It is Teacher Appreciation Week. Which of the following "thank yous" are you most likely to enjoy?

    a. a gift certificate from the local bookstore

    b. a sincere thank you from a parent of one of your students

    c. a sincere thank you from your principal, emailed at 3:00 on Friday

    d. a bruised apple, a plastic pen bearing the logo of a local real estate agency, stale doughnuts in the teacher's workroom

9. You are meeting with Taylor's parents because she has been struggling in your class. Your main focus is to

    a. get to the root of the problem and develop a plan for her improvement

    b. persuade Taylor's parents that she needs tutoring

    c. listen attentively; parents usually want to get something off their chests

    d. say whatever it takes to get them to leave

10. With which of the following statements about students do you most agree?

    a. All students can learn.

    b. All students can learn, but some learn better than others.

    c. You can lead a horse to water....

    d. Most of the time, kids suck.

11. You are making a test to give your students on Friday. What is the most important thing to keep in mind?

    a. the curriculum and alignment with state and national standards

    b. the ability of my students

    c. creating a test that I can use again next year

    d. the test must take the *entire* period for students to complete

12. My favorite thing about being a teacher is

    a. seeing students learn

    b. the feeling of accomplishment that I get from knowing I've done my best

    c. the blood-borne pathogens training movie at the beginning of the school year

    d. free Internet access and my July paycheck

13. Which of the following do you feel comfortable taking?

    a. daily vitamins and occasionally acetaminophen or Ibuprofen

    b. codeine, alcohol, nicotine, and caffeine

    c. Xanax, Prozac, Zantac, and OxyContin

    d. strychnine

Extra Credit: If you are bothered by the fact that this quiz has an odd number of questions, rather than 10 or 15, give yourself an extra credit point. You are teacher material.

Scoring

Mostly As: You have no business reading this book. Put it down and go screw yourself.

Mostly Bs: It's possible but not probable; your future lies elsewhere. The technology sector is nice.

Mostly Cs: You're well on your way to a fabulous career and bankruptcy.

Mostly Ds: You *are* a teacher. Please, take our advice and get out while there's still time to go to beauty school.

CHAPTER 2: WHAT THEY SAY, WHAT THEY MEAN

Words, words, words, words, words. Abundant verbiage abounds in our schools; and yet, in our experience, there is not a lot of actual communication. The same pitfalls in human interaction that line Dr. Phil's pockets with bazillions of dollars every year cause trouble for teachers daily. People don't say what they mean. Nor do they necessarily mean what they say.

To add more muck to the mud, educators also LOVE jargon, or Eduspeak. Eduspeak is a language that involves the use of incomprehensible demi-clever terms for everything from classroom strategies to educational philosophies. If you stay in education long enough, you will, as sure as the keg runs dry before the end of a frat party, sit in an in-service meeting and *learn* a strategy that you have been using for at least ten years that is now called something new and stunningly brilliant like "reinvisioning" or "megathinking" or "defragmenting." This will cause you to have an aneurism if you are not taking your meds as directed.

Those new to the profession will face multiple communication challenges. Students, teachers, and administrators have been trained to put things in their best, most politically correct light. We like to call this CrapShine®

and it is applied liberally everywhere you go in a school building. For example, the library is a Media Resource Center and the cafeteria is a Nutrition Station. A stupid child is a low-achieving one, and a lazy child is lacking motivation. (Yes, we know educators are not supposed to believe in stupid children. But they exist. You don't have to be a teacher to know that stupid comes in all shapes and sizes.) A crazy or violent kid has Oppositional Defiance Disorder or Behavioral Disorder. An additional assignment designed to fill time for the smart kids while the slow ones catch up is called Enrichment or Acceleration. A captivity program for the disobedient is called in-school suspension, or better yet, in-school assistance. Surveillance cameras are security monitors. Trailers used as classrooms are learning cottages or portables. Gym class is Kinesiology. Life skills class is Consumer Science and Economics. Summer school is Encore Education. The list is infinite.

Furthermore, if educators can't find a way to apply some CrapShine to make it sound pretty, they sure can crush a teacher with technical details that are supposed to be clarifying but are not. For example, the following sentence is actually supposed to mean something: "For teachers in rooms 230-245: hall duty this week is in the A Hall during 6th period B lunch, unless you have an advisory, in which case you report to the auxiliary gym for the precautionary plan orientation presentation." And here is some helpful information from a memo Bryan actually received: "12:03 will be the end of the PSAT testing period. We will then begin the day with 3rd Block (or A Lunch) and move to a 2 Hour Delay Bell." If you can't figure it out, don't worry. Unless you have left kids unsupervised someplace, no one will miss you.

While no one will acknowledge it, as a beginner teacher, you are very, very busy. You have been asked to do something that is entirely impossible, and impossible tasks take a lot of time. While you stand and stare, smile pasted on and eyes glazed over, educators and students will say things to you that you may not understand. So, here are some basic translations to help you know what people are saying when they speak.

ADMINISTRATOR SPEAK

What they say: "Based on your publishing experience outside of education, we think you'd be a great sponsor for our yearbook *The Anvil Annual.*"
What they mean: Your vast experience with your church newsletter has done little or nothing to prepare you for the nightmare that is yearbook sponsorship. My God, only an idiot or a first year teacher would smile right now. The stipend pay for this job is a joke; hourly it will work out to far less than you made serving ice-cream at the Dairy Barn. If you have an ounce of common sense you will run screaming from my office in the next ten seconds.

WTS: "You will be working with Ms. Beverly as your new faculty advisor. You are very lucky to have someone with her many years of classroom experience to be your mentor."
WTM: Good luck, son. You're on your own. And stay far, far away from Ms. Beverly. She's menopausal.

WTS: "Classroom discipline is the teacher's responsibility. Do not send students to the office for minor disciplinary issues."
WTM: My Lord, we don't want those shitheads down here. Besides we're busy calculating our golf scores from the last administrative retreat. Unless somebody's bleeding profusely, handle it yourself.

WTS: "Lesson plans for the following week are due on Fridays before 3:00."
WTM: Don't ask me any questions; just turn them in. I have no real intentions of reading them unless somebody complains about you.

WTS: "Everyone on the faculty did a really fine job last year. It was an excellent year here at James Monroe High. Let's have another great year! Go, Tigers!"
WTM: Whew! That was rough. Now that that's over with, I don't have to utter another word of praise for the next 365 days.

WTS: "Hmmmm ... we'll have to look into that."
WTM: We'll have to look into that right after I finish rearranging my desk top collection of presidential mini- busts. Don't you have something better to do right now, like teach a class or grade some papers?

WTS: "Please complete a discipline referral form completely. Include exact quotes whenever possible."

WTM: I totally love reading those things. They're a hoot. Also, there's a good chance that I'll be too busy to do anything about your referral for a couple of days.

WTS: "We have chosen you to be a part of the School Improvement Committee. We'll see you at our weekly meetings beginning this Friday after school."
WTM: Remember last week, when you kept asking all those profound and insightful questions at that faculty meeting? Here's your reward.

WTS: "We need to be more diligent about enforcing the dress code rules."
WTM: *You* need to be more diligent about enforcing the dress code rules.

WTS: "We want all teachers in the building to be using Graham's Graphic Diagramming for teaching thinking skills."
WTM: This educational strategy was handed to me by the Lord Himself on Mt. Sinai. If you do not use it, you will go directly to Hell.

WTS: "I love your idea, but my budget for this was cut last year. I just don't have any money. Have you thought about a fundraiser?"
WTM: I've earmarked that money for new lights for the football stadium.

STUDENT SPEAK

What they say: "Are you collecting this?"
What they mean: I have no intention of doing it unless there's a grade involved.

WTS: "Are we doing anything today? Because I need to help Mr. Little in the band room."
WTM: I don't value you, your time, or whatever it is that you are attempting to teach in here. I'd rather clean spit out of tuba valves than come to your class.

WTS: "You look really nice today, Mr. Gladstone."
WTM: God, I hope you're going on a job interview today after school.

WTS: "Will this be on the test?"
WTM: If I don't have to know this I'm going to stop listening to you right now and begin whispering to the girt next to me about wanting to have sex with my boyfriend's brother.

WTS: "History is my favorite subject."
WTM: History is my favorite subject for the next 90 minutes. I really need an A.

WTS: nothing
WTM: You are winning, teacher. You are winning.

TEACHER TALK

What they say: "Kristi is not doing her best work. But if Kristi really applies herself she can be successful in my class."
What they mean: It's a wonder she can dress herself. You're not going to let her get a driver's license, are you?

WTS: "Tyler is easily distracted and disturbs other students."
WTM: Tyler is a colossal hemorrhoid. Please, for the love of God, move to another school district. And for heaven's sake, stop reproducing. You have no business being a parent.

WTS: "You look nice today, Lola!"
WTM: You have got most of your girl parts covered today. Good job, dear. Let's make that happen again tomorrow, okay?

WTS: "I really enjoyed your performance today with the school orchestra."
WTM: Wow, they can teach monkeys to play the drums can't they?

WTS: "You will need a 70-page spiral bound non-perforated college ruled notebook."
WTM: Any notebook will do. I just wanted to have a little fun with the Type-A kids in the room... as well as their mothers.

Final Thoughts

Our best advice is to cover your ears and use your other senses. If it looks like crap and it smells like crap, well, good chance it is crap. Use common sense and don't be overly troubled by the fancy lingo. Don't expect to know exactly what's going on for about three years. Then, you won't want to know.

CHAPTER 3: YOU'RE NOT PARANOID, THEY ARE OUT TO GET YOU

We have, between us, 28+ years of high school teaching experience. We are willing to admit that some parts of what we say in this chapter are based on the terrifying fact that we work with teenagers all day. Prior to becoming parents ourselves, we had supposed that in the younger years, children are generally more excited to be in school, are more enthusiastic about learning, and are easier to manage. We believed that being an elementary teacher might be easier or more fun than being a high school teacher. Since becoming parents, however, we have found this conclusion to be erroneous. We say God bless those elementary school teachers. They have an unlimited supply of patience and generosity to handle the cacophony of personal needs of each little snotty-nosed ankle-biter, and they somehow manage to teach content, too. And those middle schoolers are a complete bunch of knuckleheads, down to the very last smelly, pimply one of them. A bag of squirrels in heat is easier to manage than your average middle school classroom.

Then why teach? Well, we don't know. But we know this much: "It's all for the love of the kids," is a lie. People do not become teachers because they love kids. They become teachers for a lot of reasons-some good, and some not so good. Many see teaching as the career of last resort: "At least I can fall back on teaching if becoming a marine biologist doesn't pan out." Some are teachers genetically; they simply inherit the career from their mothers and fathers. Some go back to school in order to relive or un-live some high school event(s); they are working out the psychological problems they earned while in high school themselves. "I'll get to the prom one way or another." Occasionally it's the adoration for a subject matter and an individual's burning desire to infect others with that virus: "I LOVE Geoffrey Chaucer!" And some, the really brilliant ones, become teachers so they can wear comfy cotton clothes every day, carry a stopwatch, and blow a whistle. Lucky bastards! None of these reasons really has a damn thing to do with liking kids.

This is not to say that liking kids doesn't help. Surely, people who hate kids make bad teachers. Most of us can remember being taught by someone who hated kids. Scarred as we may have been by these nasty jerks, it is generally small in scope when compared with the emotional and psychological damage our parents inflicted on us. But, the bottom line is that if you find kids at least mildly *entertaining,* you can probably last a lot longer in the job than, say, someone who doesn't.

Accepting kids for who they are is *the* essential ingredient if you hope to get along with them well enough to teach them something. Here are some basic premises about children that we have found, despite all we had been told at university, and all we hoped to be true, to, in fact, be utterly accurate:

1. Kids do not want to learn.

2. Kids can be bribed and cajoled, but rarely can they be threatened.

3. They really don't like you. No, really.

4. Kids don't care about your arbitrary grades. But their parents do.

Let's break these down to clarify, shall we?

1. Kids do not want to learn. They are not the least bit curious about quadratic equations, the seventeenth amendment, Robert Browning, or the adrenal gland. Sometimes you can trick them into thinking they are curious, but mostly, they are nothing more than a captive audience, not unlike prison inmates.

Early in my career I taught 7th grade English in a rural county middle school. Four core area teachers were put onto a team as a part of a plan designed to raise student achievement. We met every day, called parents, planned coordinated lessons and homework assignments, and met with students. My team was called The Flames, and along with your average 7th grade goofballs, it included the over-age students (we're talking 15 years old here) and some extra-special, special education students. (A local family who practiced inbreeding was very productive that particular year.) The class included Cody, who was a hyperactive non-reader. He sat under the flag against the wall and flicked at it with his index finger. Rockney was a spitter (as in, he would stand up and spit on the floor.) He read young adult novels during class and sang Christmas carols with dirty words in order to get sent out of the room. Marcus, a kid with a beard, urinated in the trash can one day when I wasn't paying good attention. They were all little treasures.

Mid-year, we were visited by teachers from another school district who were planning to move to teams the following year. They came to observe the finely tuned machine that we had developed as The Flames. With my classroom walls lined with teachers who seemed generally glad just not to be teaching for a day, I embarked on a Language Arts lesson. Cody had a clicker pen that day which he was clicking furiously while I was trying to give the directions. I went over to Cody's desk and knelt down beside him and quietly asked him to stop clicking, please. He did. In fact he set the pen down on the desk. But, when I returned to the board, he resumed clicking the base of the pen against the surface of the desk. Suddenly, the pen shot off the desk and flew through the air like a V-2 rocket, straight into my forehead. The pen clattered to the floor in front of me. I silently picked up the pen, crossed over to his desk room and handed it back to Cody, uttering pleasantly, "Here, I think you dropped this," at which the room erupted in laughter. Of course, no one told me about the reddening pen mark in the center of my forehead.

The point is, every kid has his own agenda, and it rarely has anything to do with instruction. Kids like school for one reason: they get to assemble with likeminded youth. Most do not come to school to learn. They come because their parents make them. They come because they can't stay home and they don't have anywhere else to go. They come because they like to talk to their friends. They come to form sleeper cells and plan acts of teacher terrorism. They come to get their drug and alcohol needs met. They come to compare shoes and cell phones. They come because they like chicken fajita pita day in the cafeteria. They come to find a soul mate with whom to hook up.

Kids are not blank slates to write upon, nor are they open cans into which you can pour knowledge. They're a lot more like trapped lobsters with All-Clad exoskeletons. Your job as a teacher is to find a way to deceive them into believing that they need or want to know what you're being paid to teach them. This job is, of course, impossible. When it happens, you will be proud of yourself. But don't get too impressed. You get to start from scratch again every day.

2. Kids can be bribed and cajoled, but rarely can they be threatened.

It has always been my contention that I could make any high school freshman get down on all fours and bark like a dog for a Jolly Rancher hard candy. It's fairly easy, although perhaps unhealthy, to get students to work for rewards. Like a paycheck to a teacher, a student will gladly perform many tricks for a sticker, a piece of candy, or an ice-cream. Hall passes and homework passes make nice rewards, too. Even high school students love little prizes. Get creative when necessary: "Zoe, if you stop talking right now, I'll let you go to in the hallway the last five minutes of class where you can surreptitiously talk or text all you like." For several years I made "Ward Bucks" that had my hand-drawn face on them. I gave out these dollars to student who ask good questions or say something insightful. These could later be exchanged for one point on any assignment. Oddly, some students liked these dollars so much they kept them in their notebooks and did not turn them in for points. Any reward you can find that works will motivate students to do what you ask. If you plan it well enough, they should learn something while they are doing what you ask.

Another sure fire method of motivating students is lying to them about how smart they are. Everyone enjoys a compliment, right? Students will truly respond when they are told that you, the teacher, are completely confident in their ability to perform a task. You should say this even when you know for a fact that they couldn't think their way out of a wet paper bag. Even when what you really think is that they are unadulterated dolts, tell them you believe in them. Tell them they are smart and tell them they can do it. This works on all children.

Threats, on the other hand, are a very poor tool for teachers. No one likes to be threatened. Students respond to threats in a variety of ways and none of them are desirable. From the midnight egging to the tire slashing, teachers who threaten students often pay the price. Neither of us has been the victim of such vandalism, but we see it happen to others yearly.

What do we mean by threat? Keep in mind, there a sharp distinction between consequences for actions and threats. Kids need consequences. They need to understand that when they don't make the car payment the bank lady will call and asks for her money in a really mean voice—oh no, wait, that's me. They need to know that when they come to class late, there is a consequence. This reflects the fact that our society values punctuality. Or, they need to feel certain that if they get into a fist fight with another student that they will be punished, by suspension, expulsion, or a good old fashioned beating from dad. This reflects our society's value of non-violence, uh, well, maybe respecting the rights of others ... something like that...we're not sure. But we do know that consequences create a solid foundation. Threats do the opposite. Here are some examples of threats that don't work:

"If you don't do your homework, you won't pass my class." (So what?)

"If you people don't stop talking, I'll keep you all after the bell and you'll be late to your next class." (And you'll get chewed out by the Assistant Principal. Duh, stupid.)

"If you come to class without paper and pen, you won't be able to participate." (Your point?)

"If you skip school again, you will be suspended." (Cool.)

Generally, people, even those outside of education, although I'm just guessing here, use threats when they are pissed off. A related rule of thumb for teachers is **Do not bother to get pissed off.** Kids don't care that you're angry. They will simply wonder why you're in such a bad mood, or if you are having your period. Your anger actually brings joy to their little hearts. They will never, under any circumstances, relate their behavior to your demeanor. Your demeanor is· *your* demeanor. It's got nothing to do with them. If you scream in anger, they will spend the rest of their year trying to get your eyes to bulge out again. And while we're on this topic, **Do not EVER cry in front of kids.** Not one tear, do you hear us! If you do, you may as well resign immediately. You're cooked. (It is okay to cry in your car, but it is better to be off school property altogether.) A teacher's emotions have no place in the classroom -- unless someone dies, in which case, it's okay to let the kids see that you're human. But not unless someone dies. We mean it.

It is only safe to use threats as a tool if they are ridiculous ones. Here are some examples of threats that can be effective: "If you don't pass Algebra 1, you'll wind up becoming an English major, or worse yet, an English teacher." Or, "If you wear that belly shirt again, I'm going to wear mine ... and since my C-section, you do not want to see that."

3. They really don't like you. No, really.

This brings us to our third premise. It's one that teachers don't like to think about, because it really messes with their fragile egos. That is that kids don't really like teachers.

If you went into teaching because you were hoping to get some gratitude out of it, you will be one among the myriad who leave, disappointed, within two to three years. If you went into teaching looking for love, boy, are you out of luck. With few exceptions, kids are little shits who see you as nothing more than an unavoidable inconvenience. Just as you are pretending to be in a good mood, be positive, and be charming—they (the ones who bother), sadly, are also pretending. When you go off to the teacher's workroom and call them m-f-ers, they are whispering the same thing about you in the lunchroom. Don't feel bad though, they don't really mean it in the same vindictive way that you do. And with any luck, you'll forget their names by June 17th, and they'll forget yours.

You will always be surprised each new school year by the students who remember your name well enough to say hello and those who don't. Some kids who laughed at every one of your jokes suddenly act as though they've never seen you in their lives. Others, whom you thought were positively brain dead, manage to come up and share their fond memories of last year's 6th period nightmare. Even if your relationship with your students is an agreeable one, a genuine one, the next year you get to start all over again anyway. It's sort of like annual divorce. And it's okay to be divorced. You are not their friend--you are their teacher. And they don't like teachers. They tolerate you. Your paycheck is neither enhanced nor degraded by your congeniality. Being congenial is its own reward. Just ask any pageant contestant.

Okay, okay, don't freak out. A couple of kids will actually like you. They will remember you fondly enough to shout your name with delight as you shop the contraceptives aisle of the drugstore. "Hey, Ms. Ward! What's up?" Five years will have passed and they'll stop you in front of the liquor store and try to share all the details of their life with you. You may or may not remember their name, but you will remember exactly where they sat in your classroom and that you liked them, too.

4. Kids don't care about your arbitrary grades. But their parents do.

Many years ago, some educational genius decided that we should all be regularly evaluated on the quality and state of our learning. We won't bore you with the details about where our American grading system came from or why we use it. We don't know the story. But the idea probably came from the military, which is reason enough not to use it in education. Nonetheless, we are inextricably stuck to this horrible pile of sticky goo. And while other systems of assessment gain limited or local popularity, letter grades rule the academic world and likely will until the end of time.

Grades are tricky business. You can put a bunch of math into it if you want; you can noodle those things out to ten decimal places past the dot, but surely you must admit that a teacher can give a student whatever grades he or she wishes. Teachers keep the grade book and give the assignments. Teachers grade the papers. Teachers set the weight of individual grades. Teachers decide every day what counts and what doesn't. Kids understand this. Most teachers try to be fair, but let's face it, grades don't really mean much. And, it is an unfortunate truth that some teachers punish kids with grades. In our experience it is generally the older, embittered, tired, and ineffective teacher. You know the one— he's already added up the number of days until retirement even though it's several years away. He's mailing it in every day. He uses the same tests and worksheets he developed in the late 1980s. He is prompt and does his hall duty. He attends every faculty meeting, hangs around the coffee machine as though his life blood flowed through it, and he hates kids. But he will control the only part of his day that he can, which is the evaluation of his students. He won't shed a drop of sweat while failing the kid with the 69.5%. All kids try to avoid this guy. If they get him, they try to get out of his class. If they can't, they just slump down in their seats and try not to get noticed. They feel grateful at the end of the year for their C+. We can't tell you what to do with this guy; nobody can. He's got tenure and that's all that matters.

Luckily, by the time they are in high school, kids know exactly what grades mean; they also know what grades they are allowed to get. If they are content with the D-, the teacher can be assured that the parent has accepted D- in the past. The kids I taught in summer school this year were in summer school last year. In fact, the threat of summer school is not the deterrent we believe it to be. The kids I teach in summer school simply see it as a regular part of their program of studies. Occasionally, parents get caught off guard, but in general this is not the case.

Some parents simply want their kids to pass. But others care a lot about grades, some too much. Many parents do homework assignments for their kids. This isn't cheating, of course -- it's *helping.* I had a middle school student turn in a beautiful poem, 15 rhymed and metered stanzas that her father had written. She freely admitted this to me. I followed school's plagiarism policy and gave her a zero on the assignment. The dad phoned and he was very angry, arguing that his daughter should at least receive a C because she had written at least half the poem herself. He wasn't very good with math either.

Another dad called in the fall after his daughter Katie's junior year to ask me to change the year end grade for his now senior daughter, who desperately needed a 3.5 to get into the college she wanted. Now, he didn't want Katie to redo an assignment, or re-take a test. He simply wanted me to give her an A instead of a B. I did not. He didn't even offer me any money or anything.

It is fairly easy to tell which parents care about the grades, and if you are skilled at scoping this out, you can save yourself a lot of parent conferences and phone calls. Any high school parent who comes to Back-to-School-Night in the fall cares about grades. It is widely known that Back-to-School-Night is punishment for both parents and teachers. Nobody wants to be there. So it's a guarantee that any parent who gives up Monday Night Football to sit in a high school classroom cares about grades. Also, parents who contact teachers with questions about an assignment or a due date care about grades. Any kid who bothers to ask the teacher for make-up work after an absence has a parent who cares about grades. Finally, parents who are themselves teachers, always care about grades.

Once you've discovered the grade grubber (grade grubbing will be addressed in Chapter 7) and the parents who care, it's fairly easy to make your life simple and happy by ensuring that the customer is getting what he/she wants. If this is not possible for some reason, let's say the kid's a widget, then you must prepare yourself for a lot of work in the CYA (Cover Your Ass) department. You must be prepared to thoroughly document the child's defects, errors, and faults in countless and labor intensive ways. From progress reports, to deficiency notices, to report cards, to guidance forms, to referral forms... well, the list goes on.

We think long and hard about what we are actually saying when we say a child has failed our class. Did he/she learn anything? What? How much? Will he/she learn more if they repeat this course? Oh, dear Lord, will I have to teach this little prick again?

In our experience, the self-esteem afforded oneself by maintaining an arbitrary academic integrity is simply not worth it. If you hear from last year's teacher that Stephanie's mom is a complete bitch who phoned, met, and complained all year about Stephanie not getting a B, then for God's sake, make sure Stacie gets a B!

Listen, don't be shocked here. It's not like Stephanie is going to learn any more or any less in your class than she was going to learn regardless of the grade. Kids get what they get—they will learn something from you. Maybe it will be the thing you are being paid to teach, and maybe not. But if all they learn is that you are a vindictive control freak, then you really haven't accomplished much. In fact, if you give everyone in Stephanie's class a B, it is unlikely to affect anyone's life and/or learning all that much. Well, except for maybe Katie's.

Final Thoughts

In summary, you are not paranoid-kids are out to make your job difficult. Any visible signs of your stress, overburden, or displeasure will simply bring joy to their bored little lives. Find some way to bury your frustration and just keep showing up every day. In fact, if you can get a kid to ask about why you're never sick, you should throw yourself a congratulatory party because you have defeated at least one. Good job!

CHAPTER 4: ADMINISTRATORS ARE THE ENEMY

As young teachers we suffered a tremendous sense of disillusionment when we came to realize that we were not, as we believed, trained and capable professionals, but rather minions who were told how, who, when, where, and what to teach. We think of ourselves as being pretty savvy individuals, so it took us a while to admit to ourselves where all the signs were pointing. We spent some time in a state of denial, but eventually we arrived at the devastating conclusion that we were nothing more than slaves to THE MAN. In the teacher business, having self-confidence in your skills, knowledge, and competence will only serve as a hindrance to your career. If you are an empty-headed rube, you will be much more able to accept the sort of strangulating structure placed upon those in the profession.

As new teachers we also found it rather shocking to discover that the school system thought of us as much more than teachers. To them we were hall police, lunchroom monitors, bouncers, nursemaids, skilled handymen with our *own* tools, cattle herders, clerks, psychiatrists, janitors, and prolific paperwork monkeys. As far as they were concerned, they owned us. To them, we were available before and after school to monitor the parking lot or the buses. We were accessible on the weekends to take tickets for the wrestling tournament. We had the time, energy, and desire to sponsor the crafts club and judge the Cheer-A-Thon. But worse than that, much worse, was the fact that there was a certain *way* they wanted us to do each of those jobs! It is enough to make a grown person scream—in the car, of course, on your way home from working a cross country meet to which you had to arrive at 7:30am on a Saturday. We have a friend who, as a first year teacher was asked by the athletic director to work the cross country meet. He was feeling a bit rough on this particular Saturday morning, but dutifully showed up despite his bourbon-induced illness. Our friend was asked to stand next to the flower bed in front of the school and guide runners around the flowers. As they ran by our friend on this extraordinarily hot morning, some of the runners who did not recognize him as a teacher shouted words of encouragement to him, as in "Get out of my way, fat ass!" Welcome to the profession and thanks for volunteering!

Now, there is a lot of rhetoric tossed around in schools about "teams" and "cooperation" and being in a "professional learning community." This is a nice way for us to think of ourselves, as players on a team. It's comforting. But, we also like to think of ourselves as young, attractive, and thin. We like to think of ourselves as being a few sit-ups away from Olympic gold. Sadly, those things are not true just as it is *not* true that you and your school administrator are on a team together. He is your superior, yes, your boss! She hired you and can (sometimes) fire you. He doesn't need or want your well-intended input; he wants you to show up on time every day, teach, keep kids out of the hallways, and stay out of his office. She does not want you to ask questions. He wants you to do it right (i.e. his way) without discussion. She will tell you when you're doing it wrong, and when this happens, you will know with great certainty that your position is as an inferior and you are NOT on a team.

So, what's with school administrators anyway? In the previous chapter we looked at some of the reasons people become teachers. But, why would a teacher become an administrator? Regrettably, it is often because they don't like the classroom. So, who more perfect to tell teachers how to manage the classroom than someone who doesn't want to be there? It's sort of like a cat giving swimming lessons.

Yes, there are other reasons to desire that big move up to administration. There's the money and the power. Those are pretty good reasons, we think. At least we would like the money, and administrators are paid a lot more money than teachers. Money can be a very inspiring motivator, especially when you own a couple kids who need a college education, or, say, you'd like to take a vacation someplace that doesn't charge extra for water and electrical hookup. The power thing is a bit more of a mystery to us. But we know because we have read *Julius Caesar* that power is both alluring and corrupting. Being in charge means you can control the direction of the ship, you can change policy, and you can influence the bigger picture. Plus, you get to hold the microphone a lot. Well, also, there's the thrill of being the most important person in the building. There is perhaps at least one noble reason to want to become a school administrator, but we really can't think of it.

Most school administrators earn their degrees while they are teaching. Then, they must do an internship, which means the building principals and their respective secretaries get to have someone do absolutely all the work that they don't like doing. You can easily recognize these interns in the building—they are the ones who just last week were wearing tan jeans and a golf shirt and were carrying a cup of coffee. This week they are suddenly in a blue oxford shirt and tie covered with multi-colored smiling cartoon children. Instead of a coffee cup, they are carrying a clipboard covered with student names and room numbers.

After graduation the lowly administrative intern becomes the holder of a Masters in Administration. Once this happens, he should be vigilantly avoided. If you stand too near this type of wannabe administrator, she will automatically break out in Eduspeak so confounding that you will gleefully rush off to do that bathroom duty that you've dodged all year. Wannabe administrators have changed teams, but regrettably, are still wearing their teacher jersey. Real teachers know that deep down inside they are people of flawed character. They want to be the boss. Yuck. Once they've been given the green light to an assistant principalship someplace, they quickly change uniforms and don their new, financially enhanced outlook.

Finally, the one, sure-fire, absolute, guaranteed truth about school administrators is that once they've left the classroom, they instantly forget what it was like to be there. We are quite sure that at some point before they open their office door and plop down into their ergonomic desk chair, they are given a powerful mind erasing formula in a glass of spiked orange juice. Once they imbibe, they can never again remember the enormous quantity of grunt work that goes into being a teacher. Nor can they recall the frustrations of being jerked around, being forced to sit through boring useless meetings, or being told that they are using too much dry-erase cleaner on the white boards. In short, they are the enemy. As such, they must be treated with a deliberate and tactical approach.

Types of Administrators

Leadership style is an entire course at some universities. That seems silly to us; we feel we can boil it down to the five types we've found out there on the front lines: Pattons, Ahabs, Lady Macbeths, Captain Kirks, and Stubings.

Pattons

Wearing a walkie-talkie as though it were a real sidearm and wielding it ruthlessly in a crisis, Pattons have a glorious military vision of themselves. They are always in charge of the school's emergency plan. A Patton's favorite day of the year is tornado drill day. If there's a bomb threat, a Patton must struggle to contain his elation. Pattons are efficient and are often sticklers for the paperwork. The best thing about Pattons is that they are very visible; Pattons do not hide in their offices. They are constantly in the halls, moving along the flow of student traffic or talking with students and teachers. We like a boss whose location you can know at all times. Pattons are neat and tidy, but they are neither good-looking nor good dressers. Pattons generally rise from the ranks of either the social studies department or the math department.

A friend of ours who works in a high school tells a Patton story that epitomizes the Patton mentality. A naughty high school student brought a vibrator to school. During a class change when the halls were crowded, the student turned the vibrator on high and dropped it on the floor. As the halls cleared the little fella was vibrating itself down the hall and making quite a spectacle. Girls were shrieking and boys were staring in amazement. Patton arrived, whipped out his walkie-talkie, and immediately called for backup. "I've got a code red in the main hall. Get Mr. Burns down here right away." Then he quickly worked to cordon off the area, holding students back with his walkie-talkie hand to maintain their safety, and ushering them on to class with the other. You never know. There might have been a bomb inside.

In additional to their visibility, Pattons are also typically quite generous during teacher observations and evaluations and therefore make desirable bosses. Unlike an Ahab, they are glass-half-full type of people who realize that rocking the personnel boat takes a lot more energy than leaving the ballast in the hull. They are task-oriented people who see a job done as a job done well. They deliver criticism in a delightfully charming military fashion, as in "You need to be at your station at oh-eight-hundred, Ms. Carter." Turn in your paperwork on time, say "Yes, sir" or "Yes, ma'am," and keep your hands off the walkie-talkie and you'll get along just fine.

Ahabs

Based on appearance to the outside community, Ahabs seem like strong leaders. They are large-and-in-charge, piloting the ship and managing the crew. They are frequently seen by outsiders as both motivated and effective. But what appears to an outsider as drive and efficacy can actually be a more Machiavellian perversion. An Ahab is a maniacal bastard with a God-complex.

He is perfectly willing to do whatever it takes, including sacrificing every single member of the crew, in pursuit of AYP (Annual Yearly Progress, No Child Left Behind, A.K.A. the white whale). He runs the school and everyone in it through the use of fear. He gives bad reviews to everyone and sees it as his responsibility to fire someone whenever possible. He bullies his way through the day leaving a trail of hurt feelings, bad morale, poor school climate, and suicidal employees. It is easy to recognize his building at 3:00 when the teachers all run for their cars like blood from a severed carotid artery.

Second only to fear, Ahabs see competition as the primary tool to inspire teachers and students to succeed. One such Ahab for whom I worked created his motivational theme around the slogan "Be an 11!" as in the sort of we-try-harder sports team motto. In addition to being silly and cliché, its effect was the precise opposite of its intention. First of all, all teachers think that they are 11s. Well, at least a 10.5, for sure. Every teacher does a great deal more than what the teaching contract says we have to. Secondly, competition creates winners and losers, and most people we know don't enjoy

36

being a loser. In this case 91% of the faculty were losers and wanted Ahab dead, and 9% loved Ahab and were willing to follow him to the North Sea in a leaky boat filled with barrels of flammable liquid. The culmination of the year was an awards ceremony in which Ahab announced that he would be giving the school's "Be an 11" awards. He further explained to the faculty that he originally wanted to give eleven "Be an 11" awards (How cute!) but...the administrators were unfortunately only able to come up with nine names (out of a faculty of 100 or so) of teachers who were *truly* 11s. I am not making this up. He awarded the nine 11s with acrylic plaques while the rest of us smoldered in single-digit-hood.

This particular Ahab made veteran teachers cry and new teachers quit. This guy scared off, fired, and generally offended more good teachers than a shark in a goldfish bowl. The students in the building were equally aware that Ahab was not to be trifled with. So they did what kids do, which is go about their business and try not to get caught. With cameras everywhere except the bathrooms, it was not like they could get away with much. One clever little hacker took the school picture from the website and edited in a sign that read "Auschwitz." Another witty student penned the only graffiti that went unwashed from the walls. It was a well-hidden gem in the back corner of a girls' bathroom that read "Orwell was Right." No doubt, some poor custodian was fired over it.

Sailing with an Ahab is a very bad idea and we recommend avoiding Ahabs at all costs. If you find you're stuck with an Ahab, do not apply for a transfer, as this will be viewed as an act of disloyalty and you will be keelhauled. The only way to deal with an Ahab is to fly under the radar. Keep your head low at all times, dress in khaki, turn in all grade books and verification sheets, and resign at the end of the year if you've still got your tail left.

Lady Macbeths

Women have made limited strides in infiltrating into the ranks of school administrators. Considering the fact that many more teachers are women than men, this may seem odd. But it boils down to the natural moral superiority of the female half of the species. (Oh, come on! We all know it's true.) Don't get us wrong-we're not saying women can't be just as horrible in leadership roles as men can. They can be very awful. Not surprisingly, the women who desire the move up are very similar in nature and personality to those men with the aspiration. The female version of an Ahab is a Lady Macbeth. It is important to note, however, that not all school administrators who are women are Lady Macbeths. Female administrators can also be Kirks and Pattons, but a female Stubing is seen about as often as a unicorn.

The primary character trait of a Lady Macbeth is that she has something to prove every minute of her life. She has clawed her way to the top and she is proud of that. She is ruthless and manipulative. She is vindictive, especially on employee evaluations. The only chink in her evil armor is that she is unable to quell her emotions, especially anger, as well as an Ahab can. When she loses it, word spreads through the building like a level five hurricane warning. Her skills lay in the area of productivity and multi-tasking.

She wears her superiority complex like a Brooks Brothers suit. She has a penis (in her closet; it's plastic) and testosterone throbbing in her veins. When she leaves the room, her perfume lingers as a territorial marking.

As you might imagine, Lady Macbeths are disliked by male and female staff alike. When approached by a Lady M., feel free to tremble in fear as you certainly have done something wrong. And civility is not her forte. She is unsexed and filled from crown to toe, top-full of direst cruelty. We're paraphrasing here, but we think you get it. Any minor infringement results in a tongue lashing, directed at you in daggers that begin with the phrase, "I want this to be perfectly clear. Never, under any circumstances, ever, are you to (fill in the blank)," and will end with the phrase, "Am I being clear, here?" You will dread her very shadow. On the rare occasion when she is speaking without condemnation, it usually sounds like this: *[Read aloud with English accent]* "Hello little people. Please carry on. Carry on. *[makes dramatic hand waving gesture with acrylic nails]* Your trivial tasks are important, too."

We know a Lady Macbeth so widely despised by her underlings that when she was diagnosed with a potentially life-threatening disease, there was something akin to subdued universal glee among the faculty. Teachers had a snap in their step and grins on their faces. I only wish I were making this up, but we told you, teaching is not a pretty business. We suppose it was not at the thought of her pain and suffering, but rather at the idea that she would be out of the building for six weeks to forever. Forever was the reigning fancy.

Lady Macbeths should be handled like Ahabs, although they are sometimes a bit more difficult from which to hide. Stay out of the main office. If she speaks to you, do not look directly into her eyes as you may burst instantly into flames. Nod in agreement and bow out backwards. Whatever you do, don't fall asleep at work. Lady M.'s are among the least desirable of all bosses and should be avoided at all costs.

Captain Kirks

While Pattons and Ahabs are less prevalent, the more commonly observed administrator is the Captain Kirk. Kirks are moderately arrogant, usually at least moderately handsome, and they are serious climbers. The thing they want most is to run a tight ship just long enough to get promoted into the central office. (Real teachers know that the central office is where they send principals they are tired of. The central office is where districts pile up their lemons. It is not a promotion ... unless you consider a lot more money for a lot less work a promotion.) This is not to say that they don't enjoy running the ship. They don't hide on the bridge—they're down on the planet's surface both creating and resolving galactic disputes. They are the star of the show. Kirks are decisive and fairly rigid. When a Kirk comes to the table, the meeting always starts. A Kirk wears his career low and tight, and is always conscious of his appearance. As for graduation speeches, you can't beat a Kirk. They kill at the public speaking thing.

The good news about Kirks is that they are so busy making sure things look good, they don't have a lot of time to actually get into your business. Kirks often simply do not do observations. This is not to say that they don't complete the observation paperwork. If this happens, the form will be placed in your box for you to sign, which you do because it was an excellent non-existent observation. Do not speak to the Kirk about this. Just sign it and turn it in.

Like most varieties of administrators, Kirks don't really want your input, even when it appears that they're asking for it. Remember, a Kirk cares about appearances above substance. For example, a phrase such as "We're looking at the current lunch schedule to see if we can make things more efficient," does *not* mean, "We'd like you to spend your planning periods writing a new bell schedule to share at the next faculty meeting." It actually means, "I already know how to solve the problem, but I'm trying to make it look like I have an open mind." A Kirk will make a plan, and his will be the best plan, regardless of any obvious flaw or omission, such as the entire 8th grade not getting a lunch.

Kirks do not accept criticism well. Actually, they do not accept criticism. They also don't want to hear you complain about anything. At all. One certain way to piss off a Kirk is to complain about insignificant stuff, like your parking place or the fact that Mrs. Milton lets her kids out for bathroom break 60 seconds early every day. Kirks hate this and will seek covert revenge upon you. If you think your parking spot is bad this year, just wait. However, Kirks can be acceptable bosses and should not be feared. We have worked under several Kirks and those experiences have not left us overly disfigured. Kirks can be pleasant as long as they see you as an addition to their pretty picture. The best way show your allegiance to a Kirk is to look and act professional. Many times this means pretending, and that's okay. To maintain a happy relationship, leave a Kirk alone, appear professional or at least proficient, and keep your mouth closed at faculty meetings. You and your Kirk will have a nice flight until Scotty beams him up to the central office.

Merrill Stubings

The rarest and most desirable of all bosses in the teacher world is the Merrill Stubing. Identifying your boss as a Stubing is sufficient reason to pull on a grass skirt and throw a luau on the lido deck.

Unlike the oh-so-handsome Kirk, Stubings are likely to be poor dressers, as are their wives. However, Stubings are distinct among administrators in their humanity. Stubings treat everyone in the building with respect and dignity. A Stubing understands when a teacher's own children are sick, or the custodian has to take a few days off to visit her step-mother in jail. A Stubing never holds a meeting on a Friday afternoon. A Stubing always puts out *real* food at the faculty breakfast, and is not too proud to stoop to pick up trash in the hallway as he walks along. This not to say that Stubings are perfect. Sometimes Stubings are not very bright and they can be uncomfortable and defensive in academic arenas. They also tend to take a reactive rather than proactive stance in their leadership role. They live by the motto, "If it ain't broke, don't fix it," which sometimes works to the disadvantage of their careers.

There is dying strain among Stubings, the "good ol' boy," that still can be occasionally spotted primarily in rural counties around the country. Occasionally, Stubings are old shop teachers, but more often, these athletic, charming, local boys rise from the ranks of the physical education department. After making all-state in high school and playing college ball somewhere, they return to their native haunt, marry a local girl, and teach gym. They become a varsity coach and then, after baby number two, head off to night school to get that administrative degree.

They are quickly promoted from assistant principal to principal where they reign for decades. Unlike Kirks, they rarely make it to the central office. And these good ol' boy types are made out of Teflon. They can wear bad hairpieces, drive foreign cars, fail to pay their property taxes, and even park in the handicapped spot. They are the favorite son, loved by everyone in the community…as long as the football team doesn't lose too many games. Eventually they retire and fade away, but not before a huge retirement dinner attended by everyone and anyone, especially those that have political ambitions.

Stubings are extremely desirable as bosses. Their ability to treat others around them as human beings makes them quite rare. If you have to be a teacher, this is the guy you want to be your boss. If you are lucky enough get a ticket on the love boat, do not abandon your post for any reason, even death.

Dancing with the Enemy

No matter the type of boss you've got, there are some simple principles for dancing with the enemy that, when applied methodically, will guide you safely through the frothy waters of public school life.

1. Stay out of the main office. We can't state this strongly enough. The only acceptable reasons to be in the office are to check your mailbox and to make copies. Do not hang out in the hopes of brown nosing; no one likes a suck-up. Do not go to the office to complain for any reason. Do not, under any circumstances, go to make a suggestion. Remember, hands off is a policy the suits everyone. Yes, of course teachers know how to run a school better than principals do—but it's not our job. It's theirs.

2. Be prepared to talk to your boss, but don't seek him/her out. All school administrators enjoy at least one of the following: golf, college sports (especially their alma mater) and/or a professional football team. This is universally true. Trust us. Find out which one your boss likes and keep a comment or two in your back pocket (we're speaking figuratively here) to pull out if you get caught in a situation where conversation is required. Do not talk about the job unless he/she brings it up. Then, well, you should be very concerned.

3. Observations suck. No one likes observations. In our experience students will rise to the occasion on your behalf, refrain from their usual stupid comments and possibly even answer a question or two to make you look good. If your students try to screw you on observation day, you are probably a bad person who should get out of the profession and consider a career in incarceration. If your boss leaves early, it's probably a good thing.

4. Open and read (or at least skim) email that comes from the principal's office. They expect you to know what is in there. All other email is a complete waste of your time and can be dragged directly to the recycle bin.

5. If you want to get paid, do the paperwork and turn in your grades on time. In general, principals are doing quite a bit of paperwork themselves. If they are nagging teachers about a particular form to be turned in, you can be assured that it is because someone in the central office is harassing him/her for the numbers. Failing to submit grades when they are due is the surest route towards pain and suffering for you. If you have to, make them up. You can fix them later at no cost. You may not even have to.

6. Don't be the last to arrive, nor the first to leave. This rule applies to work, meetings, and extracurricular events. Anonymity is the key to a complication-free existence. Your boss should think of you as one of his/her herd.

Final Thoughts

As a teacher, picture yourself driving a car. Your hands are at ten and two, the mirrors are properly adjusted, the kids are strapped into the backseat, and you are ready to begin today's lesson. You glance over to the passenger's seat and you will see your school administrator riding along. He is not a good passenger. She plays with the radio. He gives directions at both convenient and inconvenient times. She complains about excessive brake wear and riding the clutch. Occasionally, he grabs the wheel from you to make sudden turns. Sometimes she shoves paperwork in your face and blocks your view of the road. You'll want to send him through the windshield, but administrators always wear their seat belts.

So, step out of the car and let's review. Despite everything you know about how to be a good teacher, you are first and foremost an employee. Administrators are not your friends. Do not drink with them. Regardless of how hot they are, do not ever have sex with them. For God's sake, don't marry one. Stay out of the office and go about your teacher-type business as though you know exactly what you are doing. They will appreciate it, and you will survive.

CHAPTER 5: CRUEL AND UNUSUAL PUNISHMENT: THE IN-SERVICE DISSERVICE

If you, dear reader, have made it to Chapter 5 and still want to go into the classroom, we applaud and condemn you. If you've been a teacher, then you are already painfully aware of education's dirtiest secret...teachers have to go to a buttload of meetings. The precise numbers of meetings one is expected to attend varies from system to system, but the quality of those remains excruciatingly low.

Meetings are nothing less than cruel and unusual punishment. Teachers do not need or want a meeting, ever. You will never hear the words, "We should meet about that," come from any real teacher. But the higher you travel up the educational food chain, the greater the need to hold a meeting seems to be. Assistant principals and building level directors begrudgingly tolerate meetings. Department heads and principals call them at least monthly in order to feel like they're doing their jobs. The closer you travel to the central office the more people seem to adore meetings. Directors and assistant superintendents absolutely live for them. The superintendent is the king of all meetings. Like a commission salesman, the system CEO operates as though his/her pay directly correlates to the number of meetings he/she holds and attends.

Listen, we don't think the school system can run itself. Well, never mind, yes we do. A few productive secretaries and a good custodial staff are really all a teacher needs to do a great job. Everyone else in the building is simply in our way. Regardless of which philosophical educational model your school system is following, meetings seem to be an embedded part of the recipe. So, it is inevitable, that you, as a new teacher will at first be lured into believing that something is actually accomplished at these meetings. You will feel positive and productive about sharing your knowledge and experiences with your colleagues. But a few meetings down the road, the curtain will be lifted and you will see these meetings for the fruitless time suckers that they are. And you will learn that your "valuable opinion" is regarded by administrators with the same respect afforded the ugly girl who put out on prom night.

Teachers are obliged, by virtue of contractual obligation, to attend these calamitous meetings where Central Office personnel attempt to demonstrate both their necessity and their knowledge through the use of torrents of semi-intelligible words as well as the issuance of a barrage of handouts. If you are in doubt, here some direct quotes made by administrators from a meeting Bryan attended:

"We need strategies at levels to improve student achievement at the bottom."

"It is critical that students understand the difference between drawing conclusions and making inferences."

"These are proven strategies that are proven effective by thousands of studies."

"If it's not effective, it's not the strategy's fault. It's the improper application of the strategy."

No, we did not make those up. If that's not enough to make a thinking person want to poke a sharp stick in his own eye, we don't know what is. Additionally, at this same meeting a professionally bound handout of 89 pages was given to each teacher. These large packets were color printouts from an Internet dictionary of instructional strategies which every person in the room could easily access from his own desk without spilling a drop of ink or wasting thousands of sheets of paper. (Apparently the presenter also missed the copyright in-service that was held two weeks previously.) The administrator then "went over" the packet (Which instructional strategy is that?), out of order, and finally noted that the web site address typed on the front was incorrect.

Of the 100 or so packets that left the room in the hands of a teacher, about half went immediately into a garbage can once out of the sight of an administrator, and the other half went into a pile someplace to be tossed out at the end of the year. After that, custodians will be paid to remove the paper waste, and then a company will be paid to haul the paper away where it will either be recycled (we hope) or dumped into the land fill to create gasses to accelerate global warming. Beyond the shocking amount of waste, the truly disturbing part was that this presenter was under the illusion that what she was doing was actually useful to teachers. Unfortunately, many administrators treat teachers as ignorant and indolent, which by definition, is patently untrue. Yes, teachers are grumpy and stubborn, but they are neither stupid nor lazy.

Welcome to Education, Rookie

As if new teachers were not already sufficiently overburdened, you actually have to attend more meetings than experienced teachers do. Each system wants to let you know, in the most time consuming and torturous way possible, that the instruction you were given in your first-rate university program was not enough. You see, they feel that your hundreds of hours in the university classroom studying instructional philosophy, learning styles, childhood development, and teaching strategies, plus your 12 week practicum did not involve quite enough paper and/or listening. They want you to do things *their* way, and in order to know what their way is, they have to tell you. They have to tell you to your face, and they must put everything down on paper for you. Telling you requires a lot of air, a lot of sitting, and a lot of handouts. Many will include several fat ring-binders with color-coded dividers. (These can be handy for other purposes as well, such as when you quit your job to write a book. They also make good book ends, paper weights, shelf fillers, and in the event of an unarmed attack can be used as a projectile.)

After the second hour of the second day of new teacher week you should feel absolutely horrible, like a snake with its tail in a vice. You should feel that if you sit in that stupid, uncomfortable chair one more second you will go mad, rise and scream out, "Kill me! Kill me now!" The nice central office people and pleasant building principals will act as though you are fine, as though they cannot see your death-like pallor, nor hear your groans of anguish. This is all normal. Do not be concerned. After endless hours of careful listening and diligent reading, you will be neither well informed nor ready for battle. But they will be able to say, "I told you this at new teacher orientation," and for them, that's all that really matters.

Now, just because you survived new teacher orientation doesn't mean you're off the hook. Oh, contraire! Even if you manage to avoid being on committees, you will still be asked to attend faculty meetings, department meetings, cross-curricular meetings, staff development activities, seminars, in services, etc., a veritable plethora of employer-hosted gatherings. Each of these has its own brand of torment in store for the conscious teacher. We have been told that beer and wine are served at Friday faculty meetings in New Zealand. We are crazy about this idea. As Aristotle said, "Wine makes everyone hopeful," and if there's one thing that teachers need mid-year, it is hope. But since American schools are kind of down on the whole drinking-at-work thing, we have developed a variety of strategies to use to both avoid, and when necessary, survive all brands of meetings.

Avoiding Meetings

You must accept that, without a cyborg, you will have to go to at least some meetings. You will, of course, have preferences based on who is running the particular meeting and what food, if any, is being served. Meetings should have an agenda and a time limit. Vigorously avoid meetings that do not advertise an ending time. You will notice that when you are invited to attend a meeting, it will be labeled either "very important" or "mandatory." The content of each of these meetings will be equally irrelevant. The only difference between these two is that attendance will probably be taken at the mandatory meeting and consequences will occur should your name not receive a checkmark. (Please! If anything remotely remarkable, entertaining, or engaging was going to happen at a meeting, would this sort of treatment really be necessary?) We know a principal who videotapes his mandatory faculty meetings. If you are absent, you must watch the tape which is shown at 6:30 a.m. in the library on Friday mornings. Attendance was very high at his faculty meetings. If attendance is taken visually, you must, at a minimum, go through the doors and make eye contact with the attendance taker (usually an administrative intern). Once your name is checked off, you can use any of the strategies below to exit the room. If a sign-in sheet is typically used, you must acquire a meeting buddy who will make an agreement with you to attend alternating meetings and sign each other in. Even if attendance is not taken, do not take this as an unlimited get out of jail free card. If you skip too many meetings you will be disliked by your co-workers and likely noticed by an administrator who will immediately appoint you to be chairperson of a committee.

There are several methods that we have successfully used to leave a meeting before its conclusion. If the meeting is held in an auditorium and there are over a hundred people in attendance, it's pretty easy to just slip out. Plan your exit strategy as you choose your seat. Sit near the end of a row nearest a side exit. Rear exits are frequently guarded by assistant principals or central office personnel who are observing the meeting. Sit near others, but avoid sitting by school kingpins or any teacher who tends to ask questions. Whisper something like, "I forgot to call a parent," to your neighbor before you leave. The next day you can say that the phone call was really rough and took a lot longer than expected. If you happen to be a parent, kids are a great excuse to leave a meeting. "I have to go pick up my son. He's not feeling well," is accepted by almost any decent human being. If you are lucky enough to be a single parent, you've got it made in the meeting avoidance area! If you play your cards right, you can probably skip half of all required meetings without worry. Pets, however, are not an acceptable excuse to skip meetings ... sorry. If you want a legitimate excuse, get busy and procreate.

Using the rest room is a fair way out, but your return is expected. Time restroom exits for less than 20 minutes from the anticipated ending time of the meeting. If you are gifted dramatically, you can feign illness at least once a year without raising suspicion. Take antacids to the meeting. A few minutes into the meeting chew two and hold your stomach a bit. Then, grab your things and move quickly towards the door. It's important to walk quickly but do not cross the fine line between "a little sick" and "in need of assistance." You don't want anyone checking to see if you are okay.

Sometimes the fastest way to get out of a meeting is to help the meeting end. Most teachers know that discussion and/or sharing is not a desirable thing at a meeting. Real teachers discuss and share with their co-workers in the halls or at lunch. The universal goal of all teachers at any meeting is that the meeting end. Therefore, the single-most important rule for a new teacher to learn is **faculty meetings are NOT the appropriate venue to ask questions or make suggestions.** In fact, the fail-safe method for earning widespread loathing and revulsion is to ask a question after 4:00pm. Everyone else in the room has a life that he/she would like to get to. If you ask a question, it will have to be answered, and this will prevent everyone in the room from fulfilling their dream of leaving the building and living a life.

The buffalo method, developed by students but perfected by cranky older teachers, can be quite useful to help a meeting end. This is an advanced method and should only be tried by experienced meeting-goers. This strategy works best for boring meetings, as opposed to those that are physically and emotionally challenging. Once people are thoroughly bored they will be primed for the buffalo method. You must have a sharp eye to spot signs of meeting decay, the low sounds of papers rustling and keys being jingled. Once this happens, you simply rise to leave. If you're sitting near like-minded people, they will naturally rise as well and the meeting will be adjourned through the force of the herd. Even if you get the "Hold up," sign from the person with the microphone, you have quite effectively ended the meeting. He/she will wrap up that meeting like an elf wraps a present on Christmas Eve.

Finally, there is the ignorance card, which can be played, albeit sparingly. If you don't know about a meeting, you can hardly be expected to be there. Sharp meeting mongers will send a minimum of three reminders, at least two written and one verbal. If this is the case, forget it. However, it is fairly easy to forget about meetings which are annual or bi-monthly, or those about which you have not received a bombardment of reminders. It is also conceivable to lose your calendar/planner once per biennial. This can get you out of two to four consecutive meetings without too much trouble.

Remember, avoidance is the first line of defense against the meeting. But it can be abused if not practiced judiciously. Your goal is to blend in so well that you are not missed. Unfortunately, this means that sometimes you must go and stay in a meeting.

Surviving Meetings Without Cracking

First you must look the part of the innocuous teacher masses. Bring pen or pencil and paper to every meeting. Bring a clipboard or file folder which can be used to hide notes or caricatures of administrative personnel. Bring these to every meeting as a standard procedure that people would not expect to see you without. Under certain meeting circumstances, cover notes must be taken. If you diligently look engaged with your notes, the fact that you are actively engaged in writing a pornographic novel will not be noticeable. Some teachers like to grade papers during meetings. This is frowned upon by most administrators, despite the fact that they prefer the papers actually be graded. If grading papers floats your boat, you must do it surreptitiously. Blatant paper grading is widely viewed as disrespect, as is most any activity that doesn't look a lot like listening. I worked for several years with a woman who knitted during faculty meetings. It seems that she had met with administrators at the beginning of the year and explained that knitting helped her focus her attention and listen. Apparently, they bought this load of malarkey and this woman knitted enough scarves to warm an army of orphans. We admire her creativity and fortitude; at least she is getting something done at a meeting.

If food is served at a meeting, dig in and enjoy. Do not diet or watch your portions. As far as fringe benefits go in the world of education, food is about all you get, and you don't get it very often. It is important to take advantage of the few perks there are. The closer the meeting is to the central office location, the better the quality of the food will be. If possible, stick bottled water and sodas into your purse or briefcase for later. If you are truly desperate, hanging around after a meeting to help clean up could entitle you to the leftovers.

Oddly, note passing, texting, and talking occur as often in meetings as they do in the classroom. Note passing is fairly well tolerated, unless it leads to raucousness and/or talking. A small amount of whispering can also be tolerated, unless everyone in a large group bursts out in laughter at an inappropriate time, such as during the awarding of the Unsung Hero Award to an instructional aide. We feel that even a small amount of talking is a bad idea since it may draw unwanted attention to your area of the room and the key to almost any successful meeting dodges lies in anonymity. Therefore we suggest refraining from talking and whispering. There seems to be a wide acceptance of texting during meetings, evidently because it doesn't disturb anyone else, and it appears to the untrained eye that you may be conducting professional business. Again, moderation in the key. Follow the example set by your administrators and make sure your phone is on silent. There is nothing funnier than the ring tone "I Like Big Butts" during a meeting, especially when the call is made by one of your fellow teachers.

Once you're stuck in a meeting, avoid focusing on the pain, as this has a tendency to increase your discomfort rather than relieve it. Try meditating, using deep breathing exercises, or concentrating on your happy place. We can also suggest a few mental diversions. All of these are field-tested psychological exercises with which we have had good to excellent success:

Make a liquor store list for the ride home.

Play a round of "Who would you do?" using only the people attending the meeting.

Decide who, among the people in the room, you would be most disturbed by if you woke up next to.

Write a dialogue of the event.

Crossbreed pairs of people who are seated in front of you and draw pictures of their offspring.

Write your ideal letter of resignation.

Calculate the number of instructional days until your retirement.

Spend a hypothetical million dollars on plastic surgery for the presenters.

Make alliterative nicknames for the presenters. (Bombastic Barb, Barbiturate Barb, Bulky Barb)

While you are diverting yourself, feign attention by occasionally nodding your head in agreement. Make eye contact with the presenter if possible. Do not yawn or stretch. If you feel some obligation to actually listen, go ahead. But don't say we didn't warn you.

Things NOT to Say at a Meeting

If all of the above suggestions have failed, you will have no choice but to suffer in silence. Cracking is not a good option. We've seen it happen and it's ugly. Well, actually, it's entertaining as heck. But we feel the most sincere sympathy for the poor guy who loses it. It signals the end of a career, and, unfortunately, teachers have no other employable skills.

Just in case your mind has been wandering, here are a few things NEVER to say to a presenter at a meeting:

"I heard you were retiring. But that turned out to be a lie. I also heard we were going to get more money next year. Is that a lie, too?"

"Hey I'm paying a babysitter eight bucks an hour to sit through this shit. Could you please just tell us what you want us to do?"

"Don't you guys get concerned about fire, I mean with all that dead wood sitting around the central office?"

"You put the ass in assessment, Mr. Clarke."

"Could we have a ten minute break so I can go outside and get a tall glass of bleach to drink?"

"Is there a category below 'very dissatisfied'?"

"I was thinking of starting an addictive drug hobby and I was wondering which narcotics and/or psychotropics were covered by our current insurance plan."

"Hey, I got my raise. Thanks. Now I can buy that new can of soup I've had my eye on."

Final Thoughts

We've come up with a handy little acronym to help you review the basics of meeting survival, and that is **A G O N Y.**

Avoid meetings. No excuse, once accepted by the proper authority, is beneath you.

Gain access to the nearest exit and get out at your first opportunity.

Occupy your mind with meaningless games while you simulate attentiveness.

Never raise your hand, even if your hair has caught fire.

Yield to the Man—he's got you by the balls. But remember, all is not lost as long as there is still good vodka in the world.

CHAPTER 6: BOUNTIFUL BUREAUCRACY*

Note: By all rights, this entire chapter should be dedicated to the fine people in Special Education. They are the high monarchs of paperwork. We salute them. Actually, SPED stands for Shovel Paper Every Day. If you took all the forms and paperwork that Special Education teachers have to complete in a month and stacked them vertically, it would surely reach Uranus and back. Unfortunately, there is not sufficient space in this book to articulate the bureaucratic nightmare that literally defines Special Education. Look for them in our next book, Special Education Teachers Deserve Big Bonuses.

For a moment, picture in your mind a teacher, Mr. Burnstein, doing his job. What is he doing in your mental image? Is he physically engaged in the process of instruction—writing a formula on the board, conducting a lab experiment, helping an individual child, or engaged in a lively discussion with his students? Alas, a more realistic picture would be a groaning, bleary-eyed bastard hunched over a stack of papers at his dining room table. It is 11:00 pm on a Sunday night and dear old Mr. Burnstein is hand writing sixty-five progress reports and nursing a cup of coffee laced with Wild Turkey. It's not what he would prefer, but what Mr. Burnstein understands is that he's got to get those things finished, and then hurry to bed to catch enough sleep to be able to drag his saggy behind into school Monday morning and be on hall duty at 7:20 a.m.

We all know that teacher = instructor is a really desirable equation, but teacher = paper-pusher is more accurate math.

Now, we know that teachers have always done a certain amount of paperwork, but the standards movement has done more than its fair share to worsen the paper load under which teachers suffer. During our last few years in education, we have regularly been asked to quantify our process. Every moment of instructional time must be put into a series of inputs and outcomes, recorded, and turned in to the proper authority figure. The glorious standardized testing movement seems to suggest that all we have to do is turn the teaching process into a bunch of numbers, crunch them, and then we'll finally be able to figure out how to turn every single kid into a super-genius, able to read Dostoyevsky in the 3rd grade and do calculus in the 8th. (We like smart kids. We just don't think testing does a thing to make kids smart.)

Don't get us wrong. We think the standards movement has, at its base, the rational and munificent goal of ensuring that all kids get a good education and that there is a core of knowledge that everybody ought to know. We're okay with this, despite the fact that we don't always agree on the specific content of that knowledge core. Of course, if you're going to have a goal, you have to have a way to measure your success at achieving it. (At least that's what the people in charge tell us.) When Education sought out this success determiner, it looked to science where it saw the shiny simplicity and glittering beauty of numbers. Oh, it was so pretty, Education just couldn't resist. But there was a bit of a blunder in the choice because not everything can or should be quantified.

This idea of quantifiable operations is some (mis)applied form of a business world model where the school is a factory that produces either smart children, educated voters, or good workers, depending on your political point of view. Also, "We teach the widgets!" is a horrible slogan. Here, for example, is a Virginia state standard of learning for U.S. Government:

> Students will demonstrate knowledge of the concepts of democracy by recognizing the fundamental worth and dignity of the individual; recognizing the equality of all citizens under the law; recognizing majority rules and minority rights; recognizing the necessity of compromise; recognizing the freedom of the individual.

So, exactly how does one quantify "fundamental worth and dignity"? How about, "My class average was 87% on fundamental worth but only 67% on dignity"? This sort of a standard doesn't exactly lend itself to multiple choice testing. But quantify it we must; otherwise, how in the world will we tell what the kids have learned? We know there are other ways, but in the current climate, data is king.

Once, during a three week summer school session, I was asked to use pre-test, post-test data to demonstrate the learning outcomes for my English 10 class. I gave a standardized reading and writing test on the first day of class and on the last. Much to my horror, over half of my students actually did worse on the last day of class than the first. Don't forget, it was the exact same test! According to my data then, being in a room with me for three weeks actually made half of my students, well, stupider! I had single-handedly reduced their literacy. Wow, impressive! Of course, numbers on a page don't take anything into account like the fact that on the last day of summer school many kids just wanted to take the test and get the hell out of that place. Those kids *may* not have put in their very best effort. I did have to wake up one kid twice during the test. Passing the test was not a barrier; they were just supposed to want to do their best. Summer school students are well known to be self-motivated learners. Or perhaps, on the first day of class, the hope of finally passing English 10 was a shiny brass ring glistening before them and creating a sense of earnest effort in their little hearts and brains skewing the scores to the positive.

Whatever the case, the numbers generated in the pre-test, post-test data didn't really tell a thing about either the instruction or the learning that occurred or did not occur. Since my students spent five hours a day engaged in reading, writing, thinking, and speaking, I feel comfortable holding tight to the silly notion that something was learned and my students were a wee bit smarter and/or more skilled than when we began. Anyone could see improvement in their work and their thinking. They could actually articulate things they had learned. But, my data report showed otherwise. Furthermore, completing this report took up gobs of my valuable summer hours. (These hours could have been spent gaming on the Internet or inventing new cocktails for the pocket bartender's guide that we are working on called *A Teacher's Guide to Drinking*.) My data report, along with individualized learning objectives identifying specific areas of weakness for each student, had to be turned in on the third day of class. The ending data report had to be turned in (along with my grade book, 16 individually typed and signed report cards, and a textbook tally) on the last day before I would be allowed to go home. We spent about four and a half instructional hours completing the pre-tests and post-tests, and I spent approximately five hours grading the tests, compiling the data, and writing the objectives and areas of weakness. I'm not sure what anyone got out of this, other than a useless report in a folder. Yes, I did find out certain facts about their areas of weakness. But these I knew by the end of day one, without a test, simply by interacting with them and reading their writing. Some of my students in this class had already failed English 10 twice that year, and what they needed to learn, you can't write in a test. They needed to learn how to pass a class. They needed to learn to have self-confidence in their own abilities and to demonstrate those skills at the appropriate times. If they learned some language arts along the way, then all the better.

It is an unfortunate state of affairs, but teachers are data miners now. We don't know for sure, but we guess that the folks down at the central office are just not bright enough to figure out what's going on in schools without a pie chart and a meeting to clarify the chart. And that means that somebody's got to gather all that data. Who better than teachers? They've got nothing else to do, right? The fact is teachers are asked to do truckloads of paperwork, more than ever before, and we have been given neither the time to do it, nor additional monetary incentive. We have simply been asked to do more. And because teachers are such saps, most of us just go ahead and do what we're told.

But, because teachers don't value some of things we're asked to do, we don't necessarily invest a lot of effort into them. We have a friend, for example, who suddenly discovered that his standardized pre-test results were due to the office in 15 minutes. He grabbed the Scantron bubble sheets and ran back to his room. "Quick," he said to his class, "I need you to fill these out. There are 70 questions. Don't bubble in a straight line." Of course, he didn't actually pass out the test questions. Strangely, his kids didn't do very well on the pre-test; but, wow, did he ever have some fabulous post-test results!

The mind numbing monotony of the standardized testing movement has not been lost on our students, either. A big test is the finish line in lots of classes, including elementary ones, where, quite frankly, we think teachers ought to be spending time helping kids ENJOY learning, as well as learning to read. Test fatigue among our students is rampant. As unconscious to their environment as they seem to be, even they recognize the questionable value of the endless testing they must endure. On a big test a couple years ago, one of Bryan's students bubbled in a pattern that formed the words "BITE ME" on his Scantron. Now, here's a kid who gets it.

We hate paperwork, period. We don't like doing it or thinking about doing it. Plus, we really hate the fact that the vast majority of it seems to be a kind of faux labor designed to serve the gods of facade, the titans of tree wasting, the demons of data driven demoralization of teachers. It doesn't actually produce anything of any value for either students or teachers. It exists in some bizarre universe where people believe in nothing other than the notion that unless you put your name on a lot of pieces of paper and then send those pieces of paper to the proper offices where they are tabulated and properly filed, then you must not be doing anything. Without the written proof on thousands of sheets of paper, you may not even exist.

While we're on the topic we'd like to know, for the love of Pete, why the computer was even invented if we're going to print out everything on paper anyway? If I can pay all of my bills, buy paperless airline tickets, books, movies, major kitchen appliances, and send photos to my mother in Ohio without using a single scrap of paper, then why must I fill out one paper form to get a textbook for my new student and a second form to get the kid a desk? Okay, we're starting to rant. Sorry. But we can't oversimplify what is an exponentially worsening, complicated, systemic problem that is driving teachers out of the profession as though they were being chased by rabid hounds.

Paper Rain, Paper Rain

The basic problem is that teachers are asked to do too many tasks in too little time. Before we suggest some solutions, you must understand that the underlying premise upon which our philosophy is founded is that **teaching the kids well is our first priority** (maybe our only one, which, looking back, might make us less than desirable employees). We think any time spent either engaged in that activity specifically, or engaged in planning for that, is time well spent. Second, **pretty**

much everything else is irrelevant, overly-complicated, annoying, and fruitless.

Just in case you think we may be exaggerating, we have included a few examples of the kind of linguistic and bureaucratic attacks that teachers are fending off daily.

From an email (hope you don't need a day off):

> **From:** [Administrator X]
> **Sent:** Wed 8/30
> **To:** [Teachers]
> **Subject:** Leave
>
> Attention Teachers:
> As in the past, I will attempt to keep you updated with certain dates that will not be good dates for you to request personal leave if at all possible. The following dates already have nine or more teachers out due to staff development, etc. If you must have leave on one of these dates, come and talk with me. [Those dates are] Monday, Sept. 18, Wednesday, Sept 20, Thursday, Oct. 5, Friday, Oct. 6, Tuesday, Oct. 24, Wednesday, Oct. 25, Thursday, Oct. 26, Tuesday, Oct. 31, Wednesday, Nov. 1, Tuesday, Dec. 5, Wednesday, Dec. 6, Friday, Dec. 15.
>
> Thanks for your help in this matter.

From a school reform survey for teachers:

> Please rate your own perceived degree of importance for each of the recommendations below [on a scale of 1-5].

A. Every school will be a learning community for the entire community. As such the school will promote the use of Personal Learning Plans for each educator and provide resources to ensure the principal, teachers, and other staff members can address their own learning and professional development needs as they relate to improved student learning.

The title of a presentation made at a meeting Bryan attended this year (no joke):

ECONOMICS EDUCATION AND FINANCIAL LITERACY: Objectives and Correlations to Mathematics and History and Social Science Standards of Learning and Career and Technical Education Competencies

Here's an, exam schedule: (We double-dog dare you to figure out when to give the test!)

COMPREHENSIVE/QUARTERLY ASSESSEMENT
SCHEDULE FOR QUARTER I

WEEKS 4-5 (By 10/6): Project assignments (if project is quarterly assessment) and rubric for scoring must be given to dept. head for review/approval by team. Note: This could be done earlier in the quarter.

WEEK 6 (By 10/11): Written paper/pencil assessment must be given to department head for review/approval by team. Note: This could be done earlier in quarter.

*WEEK 7 AND 8 (By 10/25): Project assessments are due on schedule determined by department heads.

*SOCIAL STUDIES AND HEALTH/PE QUARTERLY ASSESSEMENTS ARE SCHEDULED THESE WEEKS DUE TO LAB SPACE

WEEK 9 (10/26-11/3): If paper/pencil assessments are done this week, they must follow this schedule. Assessments are given during regularly scheduled periods. Note: Paper/pencil assessments may be done earlier in the quarter. This schedule is ONLY to ensure that no student will have more than 2 major assessments on any given day. This is not to suggest that you MUST give a paper/pencil assessment OR that if you do so, you must give it during this week. Please see [administrator] if you have ANY QUESTIONS about this.

Wednesday 10/25: assessments in
1st period (if Day 1), or
2nd period (if Day 2) and
5th and 6th periods*
5th and 6th period assessment given over two days

Thurs 10/26: assessments in
2nd period (if Day 2), or
1st period (if Day 1) and
5th and 6th periods*
5th and 6th period assessment given over two days

Friday 10/27: assessments in
3rd and 7th periods (if Day 1), or
4th and 8th periods (if Day 2)

Monday 10/30: assessments in
4th and 8th periods (if Day 2), or
3rd and 7th periods (if Day 1)

(October 31): Grading, make-up and review of
assessments, and move on to second 9-weeks material!

Here's the sort of thing we regularly get from the central

office:

County School WYA-004 Regulation*
In accordance with County Health and Hygiene
Regulation 34-501, please observe the following
procedures.

1. Complete and sign form WYA-001.
2. Submit form WYA-001 to your Department
Chairperson. (Dept. Chair, see Policy Manual for proper
procedure for collecting and submitting WYA Forms to
administrative personnel.)
3. After each use, note quantity on WYA-002 form
posted on door of each teacher restroom area.
Recommended use is no more than four squares per
wipe.
4. Return promptly to assigned duties.

*This regulation must be posted in all teacher restroom
facilities. Recommended location is above roll
dispenser.

Okay, so we made up the Wipe your Ass Form. We couldn't
resist. But seriously, it's not that far from the truth.

Evading and Averting: It's All You've Got

As a new teacher you will be given a certain amount of leeway in your paperwork production. This is a real stroke of good fortune for you. Take advantage of this gift by simply NOT completing any of the myriad of forms such as textbook forms, fine lists, request forms, surveys, room inventories, and other miscellaneous forms. Once you have failed to complete any/all of the forms, two consequences, neither of them fatal, will occur. One, you will be asked for at least some of the forms by your boss. This is okay. You will learn which forms are important and which are not. You will add years to your life by cutting out those forms that nobody checks for the remainder of your tenure. The second result is that you will earn a reputation among the secretaries as "someone who doesn't do his/her paperwork." Despite its negative sound, this is really a good thing. Whenever your name is left unchecked on a list, they will simply shake their heads and mutter, "Yeah, that guy never completes his End-of-year Desk Tally." Depending on how busy the form collector is, you will likely not be asked to complete it. You can sit behind your desk in your room with your feet up and just laugh and laugh. You, my friend, are a genius.

If you are not a new teacher, all is not lost. You can still arrange all of the above for yourself. Simply fall in your classroom and bump your head. See the nurse for an ice pack and go home early. The next day, park in the wrong spot and skip your lunch duty. Thereafter, your paperwork production can be sporadic, or possibly non-existent. When asked about missing work, mention that you've been having memory problems since "the accident." This can be milked longer by occasionally wearing mismatched socks and/or tripping though the main office door. Don't overplay your hand; a hint of senility will go a long way here. Eventually, your reputation will give way to a lifetime of paperwork forgiveness.

Lesson Planning Is Not for Losers, But Sucking Up to the Man Is

Some school divisions require daily lesson plans be turned in and some do not. If yours does, we sympathize. Some systems even naively call for plans to be turned in a week in advance. If you have been in the classroom, you know what an impossibility that is. During any 90 minute block of time, a multitude of both productive and non-productive events can occur that dramatically alter both the content and the delivery of any particular instruction. Good teaching requires flexibility and sudden course alterations. All written lesson plans are works of fiction about ten minutes into the week and we believe that most administrators, even the bad ones, understand· that. This is probably why they don't usually read them.

If administrators don't like you, or are unhappy about what's going on in your classroom, they will use your lesson plans, or the lack thereof, as a demonstration of your inadequacies. However, we feel strongly that writing really spectacular lesson plans will not make you a good teacher, just as writing really sketchy plans doesn't make you a bad one. Some of the best teachers we know work right out of their very own noggins. In our experience we've seen that many of the best and most teachable moments happen spontaneously. Sometimes a lesson that is a dismal failure results in a desperate change of course that turns out to be preternaturally perfect. It's a cool thing.

Our advice is this: don't get yourself into a lather over written lesson plans. But, if the school system requires it, something must be turned in. Use the plans of other teachers, copy plans from the Internet, use prepared plans published by the textbook publisher, do whatever you must to fulfill the minimum standards. Do this as efficiently as possible and don't worry about the quality too much. Then, go into your classroom and teach away. If you need to write some real plans down for your own use, by all means, do so. Keep a notebook, even. You can use one of those ring binders you were given during pre-service week.

Whatever the case, you must always have plenty in mind for students to do. Ten unoccupied minutes left in the period is just enough time for any decent group of students to plan and execute an act of disobedience so terrifying that it can't be shown on television. Do not feel badly about the half-assed effort on the written plan, however. It does not define you. What you do in your classroom with your students does.

Final Thoughts

The job of teacher is hard enough; taking some short cuts here and there is a necessity. Don't do anything that affronts your moral code, but being a paperwork perfectionist is not going to get you into heaven (or even a nice retirement community). Don't sweat data or data analysis. That's why they pay those people in the central office all that money. Don't ever do bureaucratic paperwork on your own time; that is school business and should be completed on their dime.

Write the required lesson plans in the required format, but only if you are required. Otherwise, just make sure you have a plan every day and that you have a variety of quality learning activities with which to fill every moment of every class.

You are a teacher, not a data miner. Good teachers know what is going on in their classroom, so make sure you do. This does not require numbers of any sort. Look around, listen, and ask the kids what they learned. If they can tell you something, you're golden.

CHAPTER 7: THE MAGIC PENCIL AND OTHER TIME-SAVING DEVICES

Perhaps you can remember playing school when you were a kid. You set up a one-room school house with a small blackboard and colored chalk in the basement. You dressed up in something dowdy and gave your little brother quizzes on addition, spelling, and the elements of the periodic table. That was fun for some reason. Perhaps it was the fat red marker with which you could scrawl the big F or the A+ on the paper. Maybe it was because you were pretending, and pretending is all about the ideal. Were you to have actually had to evaluate his sad, sloppy answers, playing school might not have been the delight that it was. If you haven't been in the classroom yet, we're here to tell you that there is absolutely nothing fun about giving grades. In fact, if you enjoy grading papers and recording grades, then you are a sick, sick individual who needs professional help.

The Grading Conundrum

Here's the bottom line on grades: grades are nothing more and nothing less than letters or numbers on a paper indicating a student's level of correctness on a particular day. Your job is to put the *right* number or letter down on the paper and then record it in your grade book. What that grade means depends a lot on who you are and what you think it means. If you think grades are a genuine reflection of the amount of learning that occurred, you're wrong. If you think they represent a measure of what you taught, you're not right either. If you think grades represent traits such as a child's abilities or the amount of effort that child put in, well, you're very likely wrong again. If you think that a grade is your arbitrary ranking of what you think you taught and what you think kids should have learned had they been paying attention, then you're probably closer to being right. But it's more amusing for us to tell you you're wrong again.

But wait, you say...numbers can't lie. If a student gets 8 questions out of 10 correct, he has mastered 80% of the material covered. Oh really? Are you sure? Maybe he's a good guesser, maybe he cheated, maybe he misread two of the questions, maybe you miskeyed the Scantron sheet, maybe in his class you forgot to go over question number 7, and maybe number 5 isn't a valid question anyway. And are those 10 questions even representative of the instruction that occurred? His 80% is his level of correctness today only compared to *your* level of correctness today. Grading is entirely fallible as a system. Too bad. Listen, we don't really know what grades mean and we don't spend too much time fretting over it; we just accept the fact that they must be given. Again, sorry.

So, with this in mind, how *does* one lowly teacher grade 135 essays in a sitting? First of all, use a rubric to ensure fair and equitable standards and to save time. No, wait, uh, just kidding ... the answer is quite simple: you can't actually grade 135 essays in an evening, even with a rubric. Nobody can. It is just one of the million impossible things you are asked to do as a teacher. So, that being the case, what then? You must accept as given all of the following:

You have to give kids grades as a part of your job.

It is your responsibility to ensure that all children have the utmost opportunity to be successful. Many people view grades as a measure of success.

Grades are not a weapon of revenge and should never be used maliciously, even if the kid is a rotten despicable brat. (If you really need revenge, recommend him for a "child study" in which guidance counselors, psychologists, and administrators will pick him apart like a frog tacked to a dissection board.)

Grades only motivate some of the kids, and since you have to motive *all* of the kids, grades are not a great way to do that.

Obviously, we don't really care for the whole grade generating part of teaching. It takes colossal amounts of time and is about as entertaining as a dental visit. If grading were not a part of the teaching world, that world would be paradise. We would do it for free, probably. Children and teachers would dance and sing their ways to school in the morning. As to whether kids would continue to learn without the threat of those famous five upper case letters of the alphabet hanging over their heads, it's hard to say. We think a more authentic version of learning might actually occur in the absence of grades. But the chances of that happening are about as likely as Christ being dropped from Christianity.

Handling Grade Grubbers

Identifying the grade grubbers and various others who care must be one of your top priorities each new season. A grade grubber is a chronic annoyance to all teachers and is not hard to spot. He is the kid who is always asking if something counts for extra credit. She invades the teacher's personal space when papers are passed back arguing every missed item. His hand shoots up whenever a volunteer is called for, and she swears that yours is her favorite class and you are her very favorite teacher of all time. Grade grubbers are rarely particularly bright, however, just voracious.

If you as the teacher said that you needed a kidney and would be giving extra credit for such organ, a grade grubber would see to it that there would be one, on ice in a cooler, on your desk the next morning when you arrived at school. A signed note would be attached wishing you well. Then, later that day, the kidney giver would stop by "just to make sure you got it." Grade grubbers live to make teachers' lives miserable. They have the nasty habit of pointing out your each and every mistake and perpetually reminding you of your human frailties. And if they don't get the grade they're after, they are relentless in their persecution.

On the upside, the grade grubber is fun to mess with. For example, Bryan likes to announce pop quizzes over topics that have not yet been covered and watch the grade grubber's face go violet. Or, he starts to pass out a test that is actually scheduled for the following day. I prefer to call grade grubbers by the wrong name. This makes them furious. And we all know making kids furious is a whole lot better than them doing it to you.

Once you have identified those who care about grades, watch their grades carefully. You can avoid hundreds of hours spent in meetings and on phone calls with parents if you just keep a close eye on the grades of those who care. Also, it is **ALWAYS** better to call a parent than to have the parent call you. You can't score a touchdown unless your team has the ball. Once a parent has got you inside the twenty, you can only hunker down and try to hold the line. Check your grades regularly enough that you have a good solid sense of how kids are doing right off the cuff. Let kids know how they're doing frequently. Don't wait for report cards and progress reports. Since many school systems see fit to give high school teachers over a hundred students, that might sound difficult. Just like a 401(k) plan, a small investment of your time up front will result in major savings later on.

Suicidal Sunday: How NOT to Grade Papers

The most basic of all fundamentals in the grading department is this: **don't assign more work than you can grade (or pretend to grade)**. We know that this sounds simple, but even experienced teachers sometimes inadvertently get caught with ten stacks of ungraded papers and 24 hours until report cards are due. Unfortunately, you must give kids credit of some type for everything they do in your class. Yes, we know we told you that kids don't care about their grades, but giving grades is like payment for services rendered. It makes them feel as though their effort and involvement matters.

Don't ever say something "doesn't count," even when it doesn't. Before giving a single direction on an assignment, ask the students to put their names on their papers. This gives the impression/illusion that it is a graded assignment. And always collect students' work. If you don't collect and grade or pretend to grade at least 99% of their written work, they will NOT do it. You wouldn't show up to work if they stopped paying you, right?

Multiple choice questions are pretty easy to grade, but if you've been silly enough to assign actual writing, well, you're screwed. Kids expect their papers to be returned and they expect you to actually read them (or at least make it look like you did). They will know if you have not and they will not only hold it against you, but they will lower their efforts to meet yours.

Do not ever promise to have papers back in a specific amount of time. Tell the kids you're doing your best, and remind them that they invested a lot of effort in their work and you are simply treating their time and effort with an equivalent respect. They will laugh when you say this, and you've bought yourself a few more days.

Once you have some papers to grade, putting it off won't help. (Do as we say, not as we do.) Oh the ass-chapping anguish of the Sunday night! But, alas, the papers must be graded. Since we don't have a lot of time, nor do we like grading, we tend to multi-task: grading and watching football, or grading and coloring our hair, grading and researching celebrity trivia on the Internet, or grading and drinking vodka tonics. When you're a teacher, you just do what you have to do.

Don't feel you have to grade everything. Kids only care that you give them credit for something, so saying, "I gave everybody 15 points for those paragraphs," and then throwing them in the trash costs you almost nothing and makes everybody in the room happy.

Another time saver is the sticker—ALL kids, even high school kids, like stickers. Slap a sticker on each paper and return. You don't even have to look at them. Voila! Everybody's happy, again. Kids can grade each other's work (the Supreme Court said so) but this is a technique overused by both bad and lazy teachers, so, use it sparingly. Also, kids are neither accurate, nor fair, nor necessarily honest. Keep this in mind.

We notice that many teachers just talk about grades way too much. The effects of this bad habit are frenzy, anger, and argument. We suggest that you minimize the importance of grades in your instruction. Instead, as a part of your daily rambling, emphasize learning as the goal rather than earning of grades.

Mark items correct on a page rather than wrong. Use colors other than red, which in its affinity with blood screams "I wish you were dead!" at students.

I have always refused to put percentages or letter grades on papers; this both lightens the work load and also dulls the cutting edge of the grade against the students' fragile skins. A fraction such as *32.5/54* looks a heck of a lot better than 60% or an *F*. Additionally, today's students cannot do much if any math in their heads. So, they need a calculator to discover their percentage and thus their grade. Many kids are just too lazy for this extra step. Or, if you really want to mess with their brains, use Roman numerals. "Hey, I got XXXIII/LIV! That's pretty good, right?"

Lastly, understand the math and use it in an honorable and positive way. Admit that it's hard to be right 70% of the time. Professional baseball players only have to get on base 30-something percent of the time in order to be an All-Star. Being right 94% of the time seems like a pretty ridiculous goal for most of us regular type humans. As the teacher, you do *give* grades, but you say to students, "You *earn* grades in my class." Yes, you mean it. You also realize that it is entirely contrary.

The Magic Pencil

You will find very few teachers who are willing to talk about the magic pencil outside of their very close circle of teacher friends. Like the recipe for the Colonel's chicken, the magic pencil is a very big trade secret. It can be called by other names, but all magic pencils function the same way; on any given June 10th, it turns a 69% F into a 70% D-. It rounds things up, changes weighting, and erases missed homework assignments. It saves students and teachers alike from pain and suffering. It takes into account the impreciseness of all human endeavors and allows for variance and imperfection. We assert that education is a human endeavor and not a science experiment. Its outcomes are neither precise nor replicable. The magic pencil puts humanness back into the cold, brutal world of evaluating children. It affords teachers the opportunity to be just and to do the right thing for the right reasons.

Yes, we know that teachers are supposed to adhere to the school grading policy in a saintly Pope-like manner. We know personally many teachers who do, in fact, treat every student's grade with equal indifference. But, we believe that it is better to do right than to follow the rules doggedly. Like Thoreau, we think a man must follow his own conscience, first, before the law. The magic pencil is one of the most powerful tools a teacher has at his/her disposal. It must be kept in a secure place and used only under circumstances of absolute solitude because its use is, of course, forbidden.

The magic pencil is to be used only for good and never evil. When needed, it can be a big time saver. It also saves the emotional strain caused by confrontations with angry parents. Let's say that it is 24 hours before progress reports are due. You suddenly discover that 80% of your Honors Civics class has a grade below a C, thanks to a tough test you gave the Monday after a homecoming weekend. The use of the magic pencil is warranted here; oh, perhaps adding a couple additional grades for class discussion in which, strangely, every student did a particularly excellent job. Poof! Everybody's off the hook, especially you.

Don't get us wrong. We are not suggesting that every class deserves such a break. Some/many do not. And we are not interested in contributing to the so-called grade inflation problem about which colleges and universities are currently complaining. But we must maintain a faithful awareness of the simultaneous obligation and meaninglessness of grades. What ends are served by failing large groups of kids? Writing twenty-five progress reports and suffering through ten parent phone calls and two parent conferences will not affect what has been learned or what will be learned. It will only inconvenience and annoy you, the teacher.

What some teachers want to portray is that they have no control over grades—that they are entirely based on objective evaluation and reflect student learning exclusively. Bologna! Of course, you must be fair and your students must believe you to be fair. But to them this means forthright and honorable, not rigid. It is okay, and possibly healthful, to let a student win an argument about a question on a test once in a while. It is not good practice to ask trick questions or phrase things in purposefully misleading ways. Being a decent human being who admits fallibility will get you a lot more respect than following policy rigorously.   While students try hard not to learn from anybody, they will surely not cooperate with anyone they do not respect.

For us, it is among our most excruciating moments (other than the day before payday) when we have a student who hovers around the failing mark all year and, at the end, a decision must be made about whether a child has "passed" the class. Whatever the cut-off mark is, this kid has been consistently at a point or two above and below it as though a rock was tied to his neck. Questions to consider: Have I done everything in my power to help the child learn? Has he/she put in a measurable effort? What are extenuating circumstances? Did the kid learn anything? Is his/her parent a lawyer? What ends will be served by failing the student? Will the student learn more or better given a second chance at the class? Have I done the necessary paperwork to actually fail the child? Will I have to be his teacher again next year and how do I feel about that prospect? All these must be mulled over before considering the magic pencil. As a bearer of such a mighty tool, it is your responsibility to remember that the magic pencil serves the purposes of justice alone, and that is its principal power.

While it may seem that the ethics of the magic pencil are teetering close to the edge of dubious, it does keep the power in the teacher's hands, where, according to us, it rightfully belongs. We've seen many cases in which administrators have changed grades based on parent complaints. I worked with a friend who had a failing student all year. My friend had sent home three report cards for the first three quarters with failing grades, and, in between report cards, three progress reports noting that there was not progress or anything resembling progress. My friend failed the child for the year, but that failure was overruled by an assistant principal because the parent did not receive a progress report during the middle of the fourth quarter of the year. This young man earned a stunning 29% on the final exam. The lesson here? Failing kids is a lot of extra paperwork, which is not to say you shouldn't do it, but we've already weighed in on the paperwork thing.

Getting Other People to Do Your Work for Free

So, what's a practical person supposed to do, other than spend your every waking hour outside of the building working on school related business? (I swear I saw a woman grading papers in church once.) We like to operate under the philosophy that the kids ought to be working at least as hard as the teacher is, if not harder. If you are the only person in the room breaking a sweat, you are not doing it right. Elementary teachers know this lesson well. They have a helper for every task, and they keep those little stinkers busy managing the classroom business, cleaning up, passing out, collecting, and recording. This idea can be applied at all age levels.

At one high school where I worked, I kept getting in trouble with one of the assistant principals for making mistakes on my class attendance sheets. After earning a trip to the principal's office and a good stern lecture, I solved my problem by having a student take attendance. I gave some extra credit, but only if the attendance sheet was error-free. I had terrifically accurate attendance thereafter, once I took myself out of the process. I probably violated a law of some sort, but I did not get into any trouble thereafter.

Extra credit is a cool contrivance that you should not disregard. For one thing, extra credit points are like no other commodity on earth. They don't cost you a thing, plus, an endless supply exists. I gave extra credit the last few years for bringing in tissues for the classroom. (I'm sorry, but I just refuse to buy Kleenex for the snotty noses of young people who come to school driving Volvos, wearing Abercrombie, and carrying IPhones.) Many kids think they are really getting something when you give them points. They are evidently quite unaware of how little their grade can be impacted by a few points.

Extra credit is also the perfect reward for getting kids to do your work for you. If you are counting your own textbooks, rearranging your own desks, keeping the class notebook, or making your own bulletin boards, you are wasting a lot of potential manpower! Kids should be doing all these things. A student with a D+ who needs a C is usually pretty excited to count and stack some textbooks for you. Bulletin boards are a graded assignment in my class. Oddly, the kids seem to enjoy doing a task that I absolutely abhor. Actually, all kids like helping and many like teaching and presenting. In fact, if you get really good at facilitating student-led instruction, you can sit back in teacher nirvana while they suffer doing both the learning and the instruction. Sweet!

Of course, no plan is perfect. As far as the quality of workmanship goes, sometimes you get what you pay for. It's like when we ask our son to cut the lawn. We only expect that it will be cut, not that it will be cut *well*. There are concessions one must make when you're simply not willing to do everything yourself. You have to be willing to step back, bite your tongue, and then look on in mild amusement while feigning admiration. "Great job! Thanks." You have to leave out the part that goes, "Geez, did you have your eyes closed or what?" But a job complete is a job you don't have to do. Quality isn't everything.

Extra credit can also have its some unintended side effects, as it has addictive qualities for a small percentage of kids. Bryan taught a group of seniors one year who were particularly competitive and very hungry for points. The annual food drive for the Salvation Army was just the right atmosphere for some cutthroat competition. In a battle among his classes for the class to bring in the most food, the grand total was over 4000 items, which was very good news for the Salvation Army. But some students got carried away by the emotion of the thing, resulting in Bryan being called into the office by the administration and asked to explain why two kids were slugging it out in the parking lot over a can of hominy grits.

Final Thoughts

Grading papers is a big bite in the shorts. We hate it. But, since you can't simply say "class dismissed" when you need some extra time to catch up on grading, you are probably going to have to be practical. While you don't have to grade everything, your kids must think that you are. Appearance is very important.

Don't underestimate the power of extra credit to get you what you want and/or need. It's free, and, unlike real money, you've got it to spend. Pay attention to your grade book-watch it as though it were a really interesting sporting event, or two cats fighting over a hamster. Keep kids well informed about their grades, but do it without making a big production. It's like tipping the usher at a baseball game. You slide him the bucks under your palm and he pockets it without the slightest commotion. Identify the grade grubbers and enjoy them. They are put on the earth for your pleasure and entertainment.

The magic pencil, like the stealth bomber, is a powerful tool. Use the magic pencil judiciously and always deploy the invisibility cloak. Be fair and just. And don't give away the Colonel's recipe either.

CHAPTER 8: THE SOPHISTICATED ART OF BITCHING

As a group, teachers have many admirable qualities—they are intelligent, empathetic, generous, and energetic. But there is a skill at which teachers excel, nay, soar, above all other professions. Teachers are world class bitchers. (Nurses do give a good fight. But there are more of us.) If teachers were compensated based on their ability to complain alone, they would all live in Beverly Hills' mansions and have entourages. If you have ever been unlucky enough to be seated next to a table full of teachers at a restaurant, you know that is a fate worse than root canal. You will also notice that no teacher has ever won the reality TV show *Survivor.*

It has long been our assertion that ten dollar bills could be passed out in a room full of teachers and many or most of them would complain. "What's this for?" "Oh God, what do they want us to do with this?" "Why did the science department get theirs first?" "These people do not know what they're doing." "Do I have to take this?" If you've spent any amount of time with teachers, you know we're right about this.

For teachers, complaining comes with the territory. For starters, the pay, benefits, and working conditions are loathsome. We've already conceded that teachers do have a crummy deal. But there's something else, something beyond that. Teachers seem just genetically predisposed to bitching. For starters, a lot of teachers just like to talk; they went into education so that they could have a captive audience. If you happen to like the sound of your own voice, then bitching can really be a special part of that gift. As teachers we may run out of content, but we'll never run out of complaints. One of our favorite teachers, Socrates, took poison rather than opt to stop complaining. But it is important to remember that **NOTHING THAT TEACHERS COMPLAIN ABOUT HAS EVER CHANGED, SINCE THE BEGININNG OF TIME, EVER.** You must keep this in mind at all times to avoid insanity and other less than desirable mental states.

The key to survival, then, is learning to *enjoy* a good bitch. Yes, you have a lot to complain about, but are you really making the most out of your complaining? Are you stretching your vocabulary and building fresh and invigorating metaphors? Bitching is a gift that can give as much as it takes, but only if properly executed.

Bitching 101

Teacher bitching comes in three flavors: hobby, career, and chronic. Hobby bitching is sporty, fun, and engaging. Its goal is cleverness as much as it is expressing genuine discontent. For example, "Not that I don't *love* the helpful and courteous service offered by the IT department, but did they put a grim reaper icon on your desktop when they repaired your computer?" Or, "I know everyone is really busy working on their grades that are due at 3 o'clock, but I was wondering if anyone here wanted to compile our recent standardized test data for Dr. Beckley with me?" Hobby bitching adds joy to the

lives of others and is an area in which you can take pride. If
you put your heart into it,
hobby bitching can be perfected by year three of most careers.

Career bitching is bitching done as an integrated part of
the job. Where hobby bitching comes from the brain, career
bitching comes from the heart. It replaces hobby bitching soon
after the realization occurs to teachers that they are stuck in a
system that can neither heal itself nor even recognize its
illnesses. It is as ingrained as breathing; the career bitcher
doesn't even know he/she is bitching. In career bitching, for
example, questions take on a purpose entirely other than that
of inquiry: "Who's the genius that scheduled a fire drill during
exam week?" or "What ever happened to the days when we
could hit the kids?" Or, "Why do I bother to show up here
every day? I swear the kids are getting dumber by the year."
Career bitchers are tolerable in small doses, and many of them
are pretty decent teachers if you can get them to stop
complaining long enough to tell you how to do something.

However, the best thing about career bitchers is that
they can be goaded into a tirade—a rant so horrific and
terrifying that it will cause rookies to run and hide in the
restroom. These glorious spit-churning rages can be referenced
and enjoyed over and over by you and your friends whenever
you feel down. Provoking a bitch by a career bitcher is a skill
that can be executed as easily as lobbing one to Babe Ruth.
Begin by entering the workroom and saying in a matter-of-fact
tone something like "Did you hear? We're working on a new
mission statement at the faculty meeting today." On a good
breezy day, this will catch in the sails of the career bitcher and

will result in a fabulously dramatic diatribe beginning with the words, "You've gotta be kidding me," and culminating with something similar to this: "A fucking mission statement? How about 'We Teach the Fucking Kids'? There's your mission statement. Christ almighty. Why don't I just shove a red hot poker up my ass and run a few laps around the building while singing the school fight song instead?" Leave the room before the pile-on happens. Bitching is for entertainment purposes only.

Keep in mind that it's all for fun. Remember, no actual good can come from bitching. Those who forget the spirit of fun can become chronic bitchers. For these incurable veterans, bitching is a malady from which they are entirely incapable of freeing themselves. Chronic bitchers are not necessarily entertaining, clever, or even interesting unless you have a really, really dark sense of humor. They wander from victim to victim telling the same dull story repeatedly until they come up with a new and equally mundane student/issue/activity about which to bark. They are ailing and need help. Sadly, there is no help for them. And if there were, it would undoubtedly not be covered by our insurance plan. If they're lucky, they get a debilitating disease and retire. If they're not, well, they just spend their days chasing good and decent people out of the teacher's workroom and the library and the office and the hallway.

Chronic bitching cannot and should not be replicated on paper due to its deadly tedium and energy sucking pessimism. Let's just say, we all know it when we see it, and it is to be pitied.

Elements of a Good Bitch

Choosing your location and audience are very important decisions. The teacher's workroom (lunchroom, lounge) is considered the Carnegie Hall of bitching locations. Yes, we know your university professors told you to stay out of the lounge, but who would want to miss out on all this fun? If you don't have a workroom or lounge area, find a location that is either private or has good visibility in multiple directions. Otherwise, bad things can happen. We have a friend who decided to imitate the stroke-induced drawl of the Director of Instruction as she came around the corner. We all walked away, coughing. Once, I was in the workroom shouting the words, "Why can't these people just crawl out of my colon and let me teach?" as the principal walked by. Oops. So, as we tell our own children, please use better judgment than we have.

Just like any other skill, bitching takes time, practice, and commitment. Quality bitching doesn't just happen. Skills must be honed and refined. Practice. Practice. Practice. Don't reserve your exercising for the workplace either. To become truly competent, you will need to use your family and home life to sharpen your skills.

Although there are very few prerequisites, rookies should be aware that they are only allowed to practice on and around other rookies. A new teacher who attempts to go it alone with the lounge dwellers will be eaten as surely as a chubby bunny who wanders into a den of mangy coyotes. They don't think you've earned an attitude, and you haven't. So stick to the other novices until your name is learned by someone in the building other than your students and the principal. (With half of all new teachers leaving the profession within five years, there's not a lot of reason for veteran teachers to bother with your name until year six. They may come up with some unflattering moniker to reference you, for example, "new fat science guy", or "senorita pole dancer.")

In general, no topic is beyond consideration, but there are a couple topics that have a low tolerance. You should not, for example, ever complain about having summers off. No one has sympathy for this, even if you teach summer school, attend conferences, and take classes towards an advanced degree. Everybody knows that summer off is a good gig. (The fact that you even consider making a complaint out of having summers off goes to show that you are real teacher material.) Also, do not complain about having to make up snow days. While all the other poor slobs in your neighborhood slogged to work in eight inches of wet slush, you napped on the couch in your pajamas, drank Bloody Marys, and watched the Lifetime Channel. There's just not a lot of traction there. But, beyond these, teacher bitching territory is as wide open as a Wyoming backyard. And Fridays are the best day of the week for a great bitch. Few have the energy or enthusiasm for it on a Monday or Tuesday. But by Friday, almost everybody in the building is one baby-step away from losing it. The fact that there is an open bar on the way home is the only thing keeping most teachers from going postal. But, we digress.

Once you've got a little shelf-life on you (depending on the system, this can take anywhere from ten minutes to four and a half years) you can uncork yourself and get into the bitching business. A bad attitude and a broad vocabulary are all it really takes to get started. A bad attitude can be developed out of a solid philosophical foundation. You must exist in the world where you are right and they are wrong, where you are competent and they are boobs, where you are seeing and they are blind, where you are omnipotent and they are fallible. As far as vocabulary goes, if you graduated from any decent college or university, you are well-aware of how to feign intelligence through the use of erudite vocabulary. So with these attributes under our belts, let's delve into the world of the sophisticated art of bitching.

The Art of the Bitch

First, you need to develop a vast and secret knowledge of your coworkers. (Conversely, knowing a lot about your students' real lives is something we do not recommend. It is implicitly dangerous because it requires a level of intimacy with students that should be avoided to maintain both a professional appearance and actual professionalism, if you are interested in that sort of thing.) This will be no trouble. In fact, most teachers will tell you much more than you really care to know about their students, their husbands/wives, and their uteruses/sexual prowess. Do not use this information for gossip—we oppose gossip, not on moral grounds but because it is low art. (Bitching, on the other hand, can win you awards. Being a good teacher can make you remembered. Being a great bitcher can make you a *legend.*) This knowledge of your coworkers can be useful when you need bandwagoners and may be necessary should you need insulation from retribution.

Secondly, you must maintain the standards of high quality for real bitching to be laudable. A good bitch, for example, covers multiple areas of dissatisfaction. While focusing complaints on a single area or person is acceptable if time is short, it is not as valuable as a bitch that encompasses multiple areas. For example, an opening complaint about an individual student can and should evolve into some grand and sweeping statements relevant to all students, such as, "In fact, we should castrate the entire senior class." Then, aim the cannon and shoot a volley toward the lousy parenting that created such horrific students. Follow that with a crack about a principal who constantly caves in the moment a parent picks up the phone. Then (here's where your faculty knowledge comes in), gather in some others by posing a question. "Dr. Berzerker did that to you once, didn't he, Rose?" Finally, for the full-fledged bitch, you must also bring up the pathetic superintendent, the ridiculously short sighted school board, the greedy bastards on the county board of supervisors, and if possible, the President of the United States.

Advanced Bitching-Not for the Queasy

The true artistry of bitching comes through practice and improves and evolves through use of imagery, original expletives, and embellishment. For example, let's say you wanted to complain about, Ms. Hinkey, a central office administrator who has the nerve to call a 7:30 a.m. meeting on a day when progress reports are due and there is a faculty meeting already scheduled for after school. First of all, finding a receptive audience for this complaint won't be difficult. A central office lemon who calls meetings at 7:30 a.m. will be well-known and widely detested. Once you've found/cornered a listener(s), open with an attention getting rhetorical question. "Guess who gets to come to work early tomorrow?" To which they will reply, "Dear Lord, not me, I hope." "No. Not you," you continue. "Me. And while the rest of you slackers are bellying up to the waffle station at Shoney's, I will be dutifully poised on the edge of my hard wooden chair in the library, listening to Ms. Hinkey delineate the finer details of the curriculum alignment and random sequencing of humanities classes under new state guideline." Your listener will be both impressed and sympathetic. "Yeah. She's a whore," he will utter. You've got him on the line, now reel him in. "It's such a pile of excrement. I don't even know how I got on this stupid committee. She's always calling a flipping meeting every time I turn around. And ... it's not like she really wants any input from us. We're there for a damn horse and pony show, so she can write it all down in her fancy leather notebook that she held a meeting where we agreed with everything she said. I mean all those central office pricks know what they want when they go in there. I have no idea why they insist on bringing us along for the ride. It's like taking a dog to the goddamn grocery store. Woof. Woof. I mean, Holy Hibachi, Herb, why don't they get a freaking clue?" Then, throw your arms up into the air dramatically. "Can't they just put it in a goddamn memo and leave me the hell alone?" If Herb's a good sport, he will applaud heartily and offer to get you a cup of decaf. If it's been a rough week Herb will join in, "Amen, Brother. That woman just defies the laws of nature." Take a breath.

Although this bitch is fairly narrow in scope, it more than makes up for that in its creative use of figurative animal references and vivid imagery. It's good for a high score. And remember, bitching is contagious. If others are in the room a Bitch-o-rama can result, or even a Bitchtacular, if you're lucky. By the time all is said and done the woman's reputation, looks, intellect, everything right down to her poor taste in both shoes and husbands will have been ripped to shreds. You will feel instantly better, as though a heavy weight has been lifted from your chest. Later, you may feel a tiny inkling of guilt, but only if you've done a good job.

Final Thoughts

To bitch or not to bitch is NOT the question. If you are a teacher, you *must* bitch. But, keep in mind that it is a sport. No good will come of it. But, since you have to bitch anyway, you may as well take pleasure in it. Quality should be foremost in your mind as you attempt to cover as much territory as possible. If you get stuck, you can always fall back on money; it is a universally held belief that teachers do not make enough— even though no one in America except for teachers and our unions are suggesting we do anything about that. Art comes from the desire for self-expression. If you've got a good rant inside you, let it out and make it spectacular.

CHAPTER 9: MISCELLANEOUS ADVICE

If, by 9:00 a.m. every day, you are not entirely convinced you have made a gigantic career error, you're not doing it right.

Students are like Cuba. You, the teacher, are the U.S. Secretary of State.

Don't mess with the IT Department. They can do really, really bad things to your computer.

If you are the only person in the classroom who's working hard, you are not doing it right.

Don't dance on a pole at the faculty Christmas party.

Stay away from gift exchanges. Teachers are notoriously cheap. Always pay social fund dues and donate when donations are requested. There is always a list, and this one, you really, really want to be on. Nobody likes a parsimonious teacher.

Payday is the only day that it is safe to stand in the office to open your mail.

If you keep a student after school, you will have to stay, too. Don't punish kids by punishing yourself. Crush their self-esteem instead.

Be mean until Christmas; be callous in January, cruel in February and generally unpleasant March through May.

"How much worse could this really get?" is not a question to spend a lot of time pondering your first few years.

Don't have sex with your students—even if they're really, really hot.

Brush your teeth after lunch.

Most high school kids cheat on homework and they don't feel badly about it. In fact, they're pissed that you assigned it. Don't give homework much weight.

Font size and margins are always on students' minds. The quality of their writing ... uh, not so much.

If an employer is willing to give you ten consecutive weeks of vacation per year, there's probably reason for concern.

Buy good quality shoes, regardless of cost.

Unless your system buys them back, take ALL of your personal days. A wasted personal day is a sign of early onset senility.

If you feel as though you may harm children, call in sick.

If you can't be nice to everyone, at least be nice to the custodians. You are at their mercy.

Do not dress like your students.

Praise will get you a lot further than punishment, scolding, or grades. Only cash speaks louder than commendation.

Find the weirdest teachers in your building and then have lunch at least once a week with them. Freaks keep you sane.

Avoid the Holiday Special in the cafeteria, especially when it's served after the holiday.

A payday that falls on a Friday is the greatest gift the calendar can give.

Leave really good substitute plans, but don't actually expect learning to occur in your absence.

Two things you should always have on hand are Kleenex and candy.

If you can ruin one child's day, you can ruin all of their days.

If they give you a room without a window, just remember, your room could be a cart with wheels. If they give you a rolling cart from which to teach, remember your room could be a trailer. If you get a trailer, you get your own bathroom, which is nice.

Do not get a bumper sticker that reads, "Teachers Do It With Class."

Use hand sanitizer, and don't expect that your students have washed theirs since yesterday.

Do not get a personalized license plate that celebrates the fact that you are a teacher. Please. Minivans are embarrassing enough.

Never, ever, ever invite a school administrator to happy hour- unless you know for sure he/she has enough common sense to say no.

Buy in bulk.

It's okay to nap during your planning period, but not every day.

Don't tuck Kleenex in your sleeve; that's gross.

No two years are alike. Just because this year seems rough doesn't mean next year won't be worse.

Denim smock dresses make you look much fatter than you actually are.

Always say hello and be friendly. Feigned affection is just as effective as the genuine variety.

Train your bladder like Pavlov; when the bell rings, go.

Teachers are generally poor judges of intelligence. Kids always know either more or less than teachers think they do.

All teachers work ruthlessly on their resumes during the months of October and February.

Find a hobby to pretend to have. You won't have time for an actually hobby, but it's nice to dream.

If you ask an administrator for permission, a "no" is virtually guaranteed. Requesting forgiveness is a better use of your time and requires a lot less paperwork.

If you are wrong, admit it. An apology will get you out of almost any error in education.

Don't write business email from home, especially when you are drinking.

Beware of advice offered by teachers; look where their great wisdom has gotten them.

CHAPTER 10: TAKE THIS APPLE AND SHOVE IT, THE MANY REWARDS OF A TEACHING CAREER

We know a teacher who was simply eaten up with bitterness by the end of her twelve year career (it was a second career for her). She wrote a lengthy letter to the principal and the school board detailing the many errors of their ways. We can only envision the care and consideration with which each of them read her manifesto. She did, however, decide to attend the school board meeting that all retirees are invited to attend to acknowledge her service. She quietly received her red acrylic apple and brought it to lunch in the teacher's lounge the next day where she proudly held it in the air and declared, "They can take this apple and shove it!" It was a beautiful moment. She left the shiny plastic fruit on the table, and eventually, about two days later, someone took it. (Teachers are rat-like in their desire and ability to scavenge. When someone announces his/her impending departure, there are two paths carved into the halls. One is to the person who does the scheduling where teachers try to pick up a good class for next year's schedule. The second is to the classroom of the leaving teacher. Unbroken chairs and desks, sturdy lecterns, posters, books, maps, anything of any quality will be scuttled away within hours.)

This sort of unhappy exit scene happens a lot in education. My mother retired from a system after many years, and they gave her a little apple trophy upon which her name was misspelled. She stopped at a friend's house on her way home and threw it in the garbage. My mother would never litter. When you have dedicated your life to a community and their children, and that system thanks you with a retirement party including a homemade cake and no beer in the Family Life class kitchen on a Friday afternoon from 3:00 to 3:30, we'll it sort of makes you feel used.

Between us, we have collected in our careers a brass apple, a red faux marble apple, a silver apple that functions as a bell, a couple of engraved Jefferson cups (I like these, though, because you can drink from them), 5 different styles of apple pins/tie tacks, one apple emblazoned tie, and a clear lacquer apple on a pedestal. These are the trophies of the teacher. You get them as presents, as thank-yous, as mile markers, and as lovely parting gifts. We keep our collection in a drawer. We know this makes us sound petty and ungrateful, but, usually, when we get one, it makes us really mad. If you don't understand why, let us try to explain.

Teaching is such a hard job for so many reasons, not the least of which is that teachers do not often experience a sense of accomplishment. At the end of the day, when you are completely exhausted, you don't get to step back and admire your work. There really isn't anything tangible. Lawyers win cases, doctors save lives, electricians wire houses, and auto mechanics fix engines. Teachers teach. You must find fulfillment in the act. If you don't, you won't make it. The thing to love about teaching is the craft, the challenge, the art, the kids, and the experience. You don't get a lot of love (except at the elementary level, but we're guessing here). You don't get many thanks. Your pay and benefits are bad to mediocre. And ... you get a lot of crappy apples and paper certificates and awards. They are simply not a proper acknowledgment for your investment of life. On the other hand, there probably isn't a proper thank you. Although, I personally would accept a diamond encrusted tiara and a bouquet of roses at the door every morning. That would be really nice.

100 Reasons to Love (or at least like) Being a Teacher

Unless you want to spend thirty or so years with a boulder on your shoulder, you have to get over the lack of tangible rewards of the teaching career. It's not a very easy thing to get over, and we won't pretend it is. But, hey, it's not as though there aren't *any* rewards. We challenged ourselves to compile a list of 100 things there are to love about a career in teaching. Here is what we came up with:

1. humility
2. a regular paycheck
3. variety, no two days are the same
4. challenge (duh)
5. opportunity to receive accolades in the school newsletter
6. all those three-ring binders, calendars, and red pens
7. easy access to reams of copy paper
8. all the scissors and tape you might ever need
9. Internet access
10. get in free at home football games
11. always invited to graduation, plus a free robe

12. get off work before many other professions (good bar stools available and you get your choice!)

13. invited to prom annually

14. strong bladder

15. strong calves (but bad feet)

16. access to the flu shot for free or at a reduced fee

17. a library in your workplace

18. friendship

19. summers off

20. most major holidays off

21. cool teacher discount (employed ex-students offer special advantages in stores and restaurants)

22. the endless opportunity to improve

23. get to break up fights

24. help kids learn

25. can buy sweaters and ties with school busses embroidered on them

26. free pictures on school picture day

27. get to make kids laugh

28. access to a large stable of babysitters

29. the teacher voice; a "Hey!" that would stop a charging rhino

30. only have students for 180 days, and then they go away

31. patience, the kind that would make Job jealous

32. the ability to pretend you know someone's name when you really don't and get away with it

33. if you have to testify in court, teachers are usually credible and or appear honest

34. do not have to be a slave to fashion

35. a vice-like grip on reality

36. MacGyver-like repair skills; necessity is the mother of invention

37. can get out of a speeding ticket if the cop went to school where you teach and you weren't going too fast

38. stories to tell at cocktail parties

39. the ability to think on your feet; lightning-fast lesson plan development

40. free sample textbooks

41. all those lanyards

42. cool security badge ... can be used to apply spackle or unlock certain doors

43. celebrity; as in your name, shouted out of a car window full of teenagers driving by: "Ms. Waaaaaaaaaard!"

44. whenever someone has a big party they bring the leftovers for the teachers' lunchroom

45. a tough and durable palate; you can drink coffee that others would use for driveway tar

46. a vast vocabulary of vulgarity and profanity that would embarrass a sailor

47. free parking

48. credit union loans

49. the opportunity to buy frozen pizzas, cookie dough, wrapping paper, chocolates, and knick knacks from every club and organization that meets in school *first*

50. all the No.2 pencils you could ever want

51. a dark sense of humor

52. an uncompromising immune system

53. vocal strength

54. everyone in town knows your salary; you won't be expected to buy charity ball tickets

55. lots of keys to jingle

56. free staff t-shirts, suitable for wearing at least once

57. access to school washer and dryer if yours breaks

58. showmanship skills to make P.T. Barnum green with envy

59. learning opportunities (you can review all that stuff you were supposed to have learned in high school but didn't)

60. fitness; build biceps carrying large bags of papers

61. exam day

62. neat handwriting

63. lots of newsletters; always have something to read in the bathroom

64. can borrow sporting equipment from the athletic department to use for family picnics

65. big collection of display apples

66. field trips; sometimes free

67. large working short term memory

68. personal days

69. opportunity to earn advanced degrees to climb higher in pay scale

70. as many fart jokes as you care to remember

71. can pick up some *real* money roofing and painting in the summertime

72. scrap paper for home craft projects

73. usually dismissed from jury duty once you've taught in a town a few years because you know everyone

74. low pay; allows you to avoid a shallow, materialistic existence

Okay, 74. Not bad. We're proud of ourselves and even a bit surprised. However, if we had to turn our challenge into a percentage and put it on a report card, in most evaluation systems we would be getting a D or possibly a D+. Oh, well. We're okay with that.

We've Got Stories-Lots of Stories

An ability to laugh at yourself is an absolutely critical teacher trait. Likewise, humility is one of the greatest blessings of the job. Whether we like it or not, we human creatures learn through misstep and failure. Those who take themselves too seriously fizzle out of the profession quicker than a mosquito on his wedding night. Those who learn to laugh at even the dark stuff are those who survive.

Really, you should consider the eight or so hours a day that you have your teacher face on to be one extended opportunity for failure, error, and humiliation. It's your show, and it's live. There are no do-overs. For the kids, your error is a moment of revelry. You may as well get a laugh at your own expense as well. Hey, you're not a surgeon, thank goodness. So here are some stories of humbling moments that we think you'll enjoy at least as much as we do.

There is a famous American drama called A *Raisin in the Sun* that I have taught for years. Students generally enjoy reading plays aloud, so that's how we do it. In that play, there is a scene in which a character comes on stage carrying a gift. The stage directions read " ... a man with a large package enters." I had read that line probably twenty times without anyone giggling, but one year a boy in the back row burst out laughing. (Eleventh grade boys are reaching the pinnacle of their maturity, a point that they will never surpass throughout their adult lives.) We simply moved on and all was well...until the next block when we were to read the same scene. When we got to the line I suddenly realized why it was funny, and I started laughing. I couldn't stop. I was laughing so hard I was crying and wiping tears away. My students thought I was on drugs, no doubt. Real mature, Ms. Ward. Real mature.

I have a friend who tells a story of losing a wraparound skirt—the thing went right to the floor while she was writing on the board. She picked it up, tied it back on, and went on with the lesson. The kids stared in silent horror. No one even laughed.

Then there was our friend Sherry, who pulled a marker out of her pocket to write on the white board during a lesson. She tried to write on the board, but nothing happened. She examined her marker to discover that it was a tampon.

Two other friends of ours, Mary and Kelly, were co-teaching a group of freshmen. Mary was annoyed because she had to scold many of the students more than once for chewing gum in her room, even after they had been told several times. They were doing the good cop/bad cop routine and Kelly turned to the class and demanded, "Okay, what will it be, spit or swallow?" She immediately realized her gaffe, but it was too late. Any instructional opportunity was lost for the remainder of the class.

Of course, almost everyone has been "gotten" by student devilment. Who hasn't pulled up the projector screen to find a drawing of male genitalia gracing the surface of the board? Sometimes kids are pretty clever, though. Bryan was pranked twice in one day. He was teaching a topic that required teams, and each team was to pick its own name. A team of all boys said they wanted their name to be "pen fifteen," which, when Bryan wrote it on the board looked like PenIS. Then, in the same class a team wanted to be called Virginia Gina, which, of course Bryan wrote as VA Gina. "Aaaaaauuuuugggggghhhh!" he screamed at me in the kitchen that night. "Twice in one day ... in one class!"

First year teachers get extra special opportunities to learn humility. My first year at the high school level, I lost my entire class during a fire drill, yes, every last stinking one of them. They showed up back in my classroom later with their tails between their legs, but it was too late. I had already given a quiz and they had already all failed it. Ha.

Our friend Sherry dismissed her class twenty five minutes early during her first week on the job. They were returned to her altogether, like bad little doggies, by the building principal who discovered the whole group wandering unattended.

Bryan had a female student his first year on the job who was calling another girl in the class a "dildo." She was doing it in a jolly fashion and rather loudly. He corrected her, to which she replied that she could use the word if she wanted to, and that she had made up the word. Rookie that he was, he engaged in an argument with the girl, taking the stance that she, in fact, did not make up the word "dildo." But she was vehement. Ultimately, he was forced to send the girl to the office. She continued to argue all the way there, and in the office as well, saying the word loudly many more times. The assistant principal, uncomfortable with where the conversation was destined to go, sent her to the school nurse and left the young lady in her care. She did return to class later in the period, and she was a lot quieter.

Our friend Mr. B made an unfortunate rookie error in both judgment and athleticism early in his career. A student with whom he had been wrangling came to the door to dish out more nonsense. Mr. B tossed a CD in a Frisbee-like fashion at the student with accelerated enthusiasm. The CD veered from its target and struck a girl in the forehead, cutting her so badly that she had to be taken to the emergency room for stitches. Luckily, her parents found a small element of humor in the story.

Everybody makes mistakes. Teachers are just given a lot more opportunity to excel at blunder—three to five shows per day, one-hundred eighty days per year. But don't let the fact that you make mistakes, or the notion that that kids enjoy them, get you down. You're a teacher! Suffering the agony of embarrassment builds character and gives you the sort of tough hide it takes to keep on living. Teachers can take a beating like nobody's business.

Final Thoughts

"Teaching sucks" is a simple statement of fact. Among our friends, it was the top choice for the title of this book. We decided not to use it, primarily because my mother wouldn't like it. But more to the point, yes, actually, teaching does suck.

It is a monstrous job and only very, very special people can do it well without going crazy.

Bottom line for us is, if you are not enjoying at least something about your job, you should get out. Crying in the car on the way to work more than one or two days per week is a clear sign that you are not cut out for it. We'd say that about any job, though. We know there's a lot to not enjoy about teaching, but it's probably not the worst job in the world. (There's nursing. And those guys that clean out septic tanks. Umpires have it pretty rough, too.)

When you say someone is a teacher, you say it all. It defines their income, their schedule, their lifestyle, and their demeanor. It more importantly defines their character. We like teachers, a lot. Teachers are the very best kind of human beings. They are the kind that loves all human creatures, regardless. And they are the kind that loves humanity enough to get into the ring and fight for its success. Yes, their hope is probably misplaced, but thank God for it.

AFTERWORD

First of all, we need to thank all the people who made this book possible—our friends, a lot of whom are teachers, who gave us the raw material. Thank you for being our friends and thanks for your funny stories and your support. Thank you for reading drafts and telling us that we are hilarious, even when we are not. We would name you here, but that would sort of defeat the purpose of changing all the names in the book.

Second, a big thank you to my sister and brother-in-law who let us stay in their house, eat their food, and sleep in their son's bed while we finished this book. Sorry for all the dog hair. We love you guys!

Third, thank you to all of those teachers who care enough about kids' learning to put up with all the crap dished out by the public school system. We had good teachers ourselves, ones who taught us to love reading and learning, ones who made us memorize stuff that we can still spout off, even when drinking, and ones who modeled what it means to be both thinking and caring people.

Thank you,
CBW and BWB

28217345R00068

Made in the USA
Lexington, KY
09 December 2013